## Praise for
### *Retire Retirement*

"Get ready to toss out your old ideas about retirement! Tammy Erickson's *Retire Retirement* highlights the rich array of exciting opportunities baby boomers are creating with their sustained vitality and hard-won insight."

> —Michael Watkins, Professor of General Management, IMD;
> founding partner, Genesis Advisers; and author of
> *The First 90 Days*

"In her wonderfully graceful and upbeat voice, Erickson talks directly to a generation about their hopes, their dreams, and their aspirations. With a keen eye to the future and rich stories, insights, and questions, this book is a must-have resource for every baby boomer who aspires to make the very best of the 'thirty-year bonus.'"

> —Lynda Gratton, professor at the London Business School
> and author of *Hot Spots: Why Some Organisations and Teams
> Buzz with Energy—and Others Don't*

"The future for Boomers is filled with X'ers, Y's, and unprecedented opportunities. *Retire Retirement* is a practical, engaging, and rigorous guide to navigating the changes and charting a path through the second twenty-five years of our careers."

> —John W. Boudreau, professor and Research Director,
> Center for Effective Organizations at the University of
> Southern California, and coauthor of *Beyond HR: The New Science
> of Human Capital*

"Tammy Erickson brilliantly weaves together the current and future social, economic, and vocational benefits to Boomers resulting from the convergence of several shifting cultural phenomena. Informative and inspirational, this book is a must-read for professionals at all career stages."

> —Beverly Edgehill, President and CEO, The Partnership, Inc.

"Those of us in *middlescence* see ourselves throughout this book as it lays out options for our career and life choices that will help us find personal fulfillment and organizational success. Erickson's ideas help us shift from being overwhelmed by or afraid of the new realities to making informed choices that enrich our personal and professional lives."

> —Dave Ulrich, professor at the Ross School of Business,
> University of Michigan; Partner, The RBL Group;
> and coauthor of *Leadership Brand*

"For anyone who needs to understand how generational differences influence how we live, work, learn, think, and— yes—even *retire*, this book should be required reading. Speaking as someone Erickson refers to as a 'Traditionalist,' this book has provided me with powerful insights into myself, my children, my students, and so many of my friends and those leaders experiencing the challenge of working with and leading different generations."

> —Warren Bennis, University Professor, University of
> Southern California, and coauthor of *Judgment: How Winning
> Leaders Make Great Calls*

"Tammy Erickson paints a remarkable landscape of the opportunities awaiting Boomers. Her book is an engaging, pragmatic, and inspiring guide to rethinking your career. Put this book at the top of your reading list!"

—Jay A. Conger, professor at Claremont McKenna College
and the London Business School

RETIRE
# Retirement

**Also by Tamara Erickson**

*Workforce Crisis: How to Beat the Coming Shortage of Skills and Talent*
(with Ken Dychtwald and Robert Morison)

*Third Generation R&D: Managing the Link to Corporate Strategy*
(with Philip A. Roussel and Kamal N. Saad)

# RETIRE
# Retirement

Career Strategies for the
Boomer Generation

## Tamara Erickson

Harvard Business Press
Boston, Massachusetts

Library of Congress Cataloging-in-Publication Data
Erickson, Tamara J., 1954–
    Retire retirement: career strategies for the boomer generation / Tamara Erickson.
       p.      cm.
    ISBN-13: 978-1-4221-2059-0
    1. Vocational guidance—United States. 2. Baby boom generation—Employment—
United States. 3. Older people—Employment. 4. Career changes. I. Title.
    HF5382.5.U5E75   2007
    650.1—dc22

*To Ken Dychtwald and Bob Morison*

*With whom I set off on this ambitious journey*

*to understand the changing workforce*


*Beginning as colleagues—*

*becoming friends along the way*

# CONTENTS

# ACKNOWLEDGMENTS

This book owes its origin to three creative and enthusiastic friends from Harvard Business School Publishing: Kirsten Sandberg, Executive Editor; Julie Devoll, Senior Publicist; and Angelia Herrin, Executive Director of New Business Development. Together they came up with the concept of a series of books focusing on each workforce generation and have provided support and encouragement along this first step of the way. Thank you to them and to the entire team at HBSP, especially Monica Jainschigg for her insightful edits, Ellen Peebles for her editorial work on the *HBR* articles that catalyzed this book, and the talented team at HBSP Online, especially my editor Jimmy Guterman; I love working with you all.

Much of the research underpinning this book was conducted in partnership with Ken Dychtwald, president of Age Wave; Bob Morison, director of research at The Concours Institute, now a member of BSG Alliance; and a wonderful team of colleagues from both firms. Although I deeply appreciate the contributions of many colleagues who participated in the research over the years, I'd like in particular to thank Tim Bevins of The Concours Institute and David Baxter of Age Wave. Maggie Hentschel was instrumental in conducting research specifically for this book—effective, enthusiastic, and understanding. I thank them all.

My understanding of the issues surrounding the changing workforce has been greatly enhanced by many valued colleagues and friends. Lynda Gratton, a good friend and frequent research collaborator, was instrumental in developing my understanding of the role of unique experiences in the creation of employee engagement and intricacies of personal networks. Tom Malone, Paul Saffo, Linda Stone, and Ellen Galinski all shared their unique perspectives on the changing world of work. Spending time with Peter Drucker, and trying to absorb a fraction of his insight into the trends affecting the last century and this one going forward, was a privilege and a pleasure I will never forget.

Ron Christman, founder of The Concours Group and now chairman of BSG Concours, a BSG Alliance Company, provided invaluable support and encouragement for this work. I thank him deeply for the flexibility that made it possible for me to work on this book, the friendship, and the reminder that a good joke goes a long way in life.

Sharon Randall, director of operations for The Concours Institute, is both a cherished friend and integral part of my work. Her support in so many ways is greatly appreciated.

Special thanks go to the wonderful Y's in my life, David and Kate. They give me great joy each day—as well as frequent opportunities to learn more about the perspectives of their generation.

Finally, many thanks—for years of support and laughter—to my favorite Boomer, Tom.

# RETIRE
# Retirement

# Introduction

You lucky Boomers! Blessed with so many firsts over your life—the prospect of a childhood in the suburbs, career opportunities for women, sexual freedom, prolonged periods of prosperity—and now entering a next great stage of life with several strong gusts of wind blowing at your back.

The economic opportunities you face are unprecedented. The employment numbers tell an amazing story: beginning now, and continuing for the rest of your lives, the gap between the number of people who will be available to work and the demand for workers, particularly those with skills and experience, will continue to widen. Even with short-term economic ups and downs, if you want to continue to work, you will almost certainly be welcome to do so. You have a nearly guaranteed market for your skills and energy—if you decide to remain an active member of the workforce.

This change in the raw numbers brings a shift in power—those of you who want to work will have the option of reshaping your relationship with those who seek to employ you. The tightening talent pool presents an important opportunity to rethink the relationship between individuals and the organizations of work.

And you will almost certainly want to "work"—whether for pay, in barter, or in service to others—because you will have so much time to do so. You will be the first generation to enjoy a dramatically new life stage—a significant period of healthy, active non-childrearing adult life. Advances in health care, and resultant changes in life expectancy, will give you time that no other generation has yet had. By the time their children left home, members of past generations were largely "old"—ready to slow down. When your children are adults, most of you Boomers will still be essentially "young"—and full of capabilities and energy.

Your long lives will be blessed by an unexpected dividend: your children love you like no generation has ever loved their parents before. In 1974, more than 40 percent of Boomers said they'd be better off without parents. Today, 90 percent of teens report being *very* close to their parents—an extraordinary change in the fabric of intergenerational relationships in an astonishingly short time.[1] Your children expect to retain close parental bonds even after leaving home and, of course, for most of you, that's wonderful news. The nature of relationships—both within your family as well as around the world—has undergone a major change, presenting options for social communities that your parents would never have imagined.

You are the Boomers. You represent nearly one-third of all Americans living today—a population 76 million strong born between 1946 and 1964—and a similar proportion of the populations of Europe, Canada, Australia, and Japan.[2] The fertile period of your births was sandwiched between the baby busts of the Depression and World War II and the Vietnam era. The number of births in the United States jumped from 2.8 million in 1945 (at the height of World War II) to 3.4 million as the boom began. At such numbers, you have repeatedly reshaped life in much of the world. Your influence will continue for decades to come.

How you harness your future decades of productive capacity—whether in traditional "work" or in a less conventional application of your skills—is your choice. This is the time to explore the possibilities . . . and prepare to make the most of this promising third phase—after adolescence and the traditional span of adult working years—of your life. For many of you, this phase will prove as different from the life you've led for the past thirty years as that life was from your adolescence. The wide array of choices that are opening to you, coupled with—at least for some of you— the desire to try something different, presents a series of career strategy challenges that previous generations have not faced.

The ever-prescient Peter Drucker alerted us to the growing importance of choice—and the option for a second or third entire career—in his 2000 essay on what he saw as this century's revolution in human affairs:

> In a few hundred years, when the history of our time will be written from a long-term perspective, it is likely that the most important event historians will see is not technology, not the Internet, not e-commerce. It is an unprecedented change in the human condition. For the first time—literally—substantial and rapidly growing numbers of people have choices. For the first time, they will have to manage themselves. And society is totally unprepared for it . . .
>
> Throughout history, practically nobody had choices . . . Now suddenly a large number of people have choices. What is more, they will have more than one career, because the working life span of people is now close to 60 years—three times what it was in 1900.[3]

This book is about making choices and developing a career strategy for the rest of your life. It begins by setting the stage: discussing the generational preferences that will factor into the choices you make, and shifts in our world that are fundamentally recasting your options. It highlights the new possibilities—and practical approaches to sort through them.

Herminia Ibarra, a professor of organizational behavior at INSEAD, has suggested that there are two levels of thinking that lie below our ultimate choices about how we spend our time (see figure I-1). The specific tasks we take on and the organizations we join are the visible results of our decisions. But these decisions rest on a set of personal values and motivations—factors that shape our ultimate choices and tend to remain with us throughout our adult life, constants from job to job and company to company. These include both our basic competencies and our

**FIGURE I-1**

## Career decision criteria

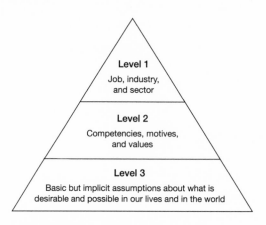

Level 1
Job, industry,
and sector

Level 2
Competencies, motives,
and values

Level 3
Basic but implicit assumptions about what is
desirable and possible in our lives and in the world

*Source:* Herminia Ibarra, *Working Identity: Unconventional Strategies for Reinventing Your Career* (Boston: Harvard Business School Press, 2003). Used with permission.

work-related preferences.[4] I'll talk about these as our *Life Lures*. MIT professor Edgar Schein a developed a similar concept that he calls our *career anchors*—the values we would be unwilling to give up if forced to make a choice.[5]

These considerations, in turn, are both enabled and constrained by a critically important baseline—our level of understanding about the world and the options it holds. Ibarra describes this level as "basic but implicit assumptions about what is desirable and possible in our lives and in the world."[6] To a large extent, these assumptions—and the way they recast our ultimate choices—are the foundation of this book.

Before we delve into assumptions about how the world is changing, I'll ask you to consider first the assumptions you already hold about how the world works. Building on research on generational patterns and preferences, chapter 1 of this book traces the evolution and underlying rationale of the lens through which many Boomers view the world today—and why Boomers' perspective is different from that of individuals in other generations. As you explore possibilities and shape a career strategy for this third phase of your life, this unique lens will influence how the world looks to you and how you interact with others. Understanding the outlook of other generations will make it easier to participate in this multigenerational world.

In chapter 2, I'll encourage you to reexamine several core assumptions about what the world might be like over the next three to four decades—and to re-imagine what your life might be like. Many of us tend to plan for the future based on the patterns previous generations have followed. For you, that would be a huge mistake—your third phase will almost certainly be vastly different from your parents' later life.

I also hope I'll convince you that the future is not quite as foreboding as some would lead you to believe. Your life choices—the options that are both desirable and possible—are being transformed in four fundamental and exciting ways: prolonged economic opportunity, new ways of working, a life stage your parents and grandparents never experienced, and positive relationships with profound implications for the social relationships you will enjoy going forward. I hope you'll come away from this book with a substantial shift in the foundation for your thinking about the remaining years of your life and the role of work within it. The possibilities Boomers face are substantially different—broader, richer, more diverse—than the options faced by any previous generation.

While many of your future choices may relate to personal satisfaction, there is also the likely promise of a generation of talented, energetic Boomers—with much more discretionary time than they've ever had before—doing good. The possibility for almost unlimited social and business contribution lies in Boomers' need for creativity and lifelong learning, for competition and productivity, for authentic and intimate relationships, for spiritual growth and personal expression, and for both adventure as well as community.

Going forward, as an increasing array of possibilities unfolds, you will need ways to sift through your options in pursuit of a rewarding life and, for many of you, a continuing career. The core work options themselves, on the surface, are straightforward: you may want to stay where you are, but substantially renegotiate the terms of your work relationship, or you may want to do something new—to use the gift of time for reinvention. You may want to concentrate your efforts primarily in one core area or develop a mosaic of activities that include paid work, volunteer work, learning activities, leisure pursuits, and family-based time. The attractiveness and feasibility of each are what is changing.

We'll look at the strategies you might choose. Strategy *is*, in essence, about choice—about choosing a path and selecting where to invest your energy and time. The trick with any strategy is determining *how* to make the choices—what criteria to use in separating good ideas—the ones that are best for you—from all the rest. In chapter 3, we'll look at two frameworks for developing your own criteria for making career choices:

- *Career Curve:* The intensity and ambition we each have for work vary. The amount of time you'd like to devote to work is one piece of the picture. But there are also important issues to consider related to the degree of challenge and responsibility that feel right for you at this point, the complexity or variety inherent in the life you're creating, and the bottom line economic reality—the importance of income in shaping your future choices. Having a better understanding of where you are on your own personal Career Curve will give you insight into which options are most attractive and practical, as well as the factors that underlie that evaluation.

- *Life Lure:* Similarly, what attracts each of us to work also varies. Some of you are excited by being part of a team; others when you tackle challenging projects; and still others when you make steady, upward progress. Unfortunately, if you're like roughly 80 percent of the people in today's workforce, you haven't had the pleasure of being deeply engaged in your work experience very often or at all during your first career. Now's the time to change that. In this framework, we'll look at which elements of the work experience engage you. If at all possible, in your next stage, you'll find work that you deeply enjoy—whether for the social connections it brings, the sense of legacy, the flexibility or independence, or whatever other element of the overall work experience you find most rewarding.

These frameworks together will encourage you to reflect on aspects of your future options that the research that underpins this book has shown to be central to individuals' satisfaction with and enjoyment of work. Think of them as a lens that you might look through to view each option as it comes along—different perspectives viewed and evaluated in real time.

Herminia Ibarra's research has suggested the importance of having relevant ways to evaluate new experiences in real time, as we move forward: "Identities change in practice, as we start doing new things (*crafting experiments*), interacting with different people (*shifting connections*), and reinterpreting our life stories through the lens of the emerging possibilities (*making sense*)."[7] Holding each possibility up as it comes along—to view it through the lens of your personal criteria—is one way of making sense.

Finally, chapters 4 and 5 look at some of the specific possibilities that are likely to open to you in the years ahead. If you would like to stay close to your current work, there are options that you might begin exploring today, including negotiating for lateral moves; cyclic or episodic work; and work measures based on the task you do, rather than the time you spend. More and more new work arrangements are becoming available; in chapter 4 we'll explore what's reasonable to ask for—and to expect.

If you opt to shift away from your first career into a different role—to reinvent—the options are broad. You may want to learn a new profession, launch a whole new career, start a business, or apply business skills to social or volunteer work. As you shift into this third phase of life, you are likely to have more time and greater leverage than have been available to you in the past to achieve whatever goals you set. In chapter 5, we'll look at how you can experiment, network, prepare, and build on your success as you move ahead.

This book offers you a chance to step back and take a fresh look at your career. The topic is timely, since you are moving toward traditional retirement age. But rather than bowing out of the work world, as a Boomer today you have a unique opportunity to think about what you want and how you will get it. You have *time*—and the changing world is offering you new opportunities.

Unlike those of many other authors, you'll find that my point of view is fundamentally optimistic. Of course there are challenges—and other authors cover these in depth. There are also great possibilities ahead. You need to begin today to explore opportunities that will fit your unique needs and preferences—for the next thirty years.

This is a book for you.

CHAPTER ONE

# Why Do You Think
# What You Think?

Have you ever noticed that a lot of the advertisements aimed at Boomers feature music or other symbols of the 1960s? Wondered why?

Marketers have known for some time that many of our most powerful impressions were formed when we were teenagers—when we emerged from our inwardly focused childhood and looked out at the world around us. What we saw at that moment, in the world and in our families, formed an indelible impression of how the world works—and determined for life what we cared most about.

It turns out these same teenage impressions not only shape our assumptions about the world, but also about the role of work within it.[1]

Think for a minute about the 1950s—a time when people who are in their sixties today would have been teens. In the booming postwar economies of Europe and America, opportunity appeared on every street corner. Suburbs were popping up, and the dream of home ownership seemed suddenly in reach. Factories that had made war machines were cranking out washing machines at an astounding rate. Consumer purchases skyrocketed.

Now, imagine you're a teenager "waking up" in that moment. What assumptions would you form about how the world works? Whom would you respect and trust? What would you expect to do with your life? How would you measure its success?

Any one answer to these questions is, of course, a bit of a generalization—stretching to capture the common characteristics of people in many different circumstances. But, for most who grew up in this economy of grand promise and endless optimism, the assumptions formed turn out to be remarkably similar. A logical desire for any teen of this era would have been to leap enthusiastically into the work world as it existed then—to get a piece of the pie. Corporate leaders and government officials warranted respect. And financial success became more than a respectable life goal—for many it also became a symbol, a measure of the degree to which that teenage desire for a piece of the pie had come to pass.

These perspectives changed radically in the 1960s and 1970s, and again in the following decades, yielding generations with dramatically different expectations—about the type of relationships individuals form with corporations, peers, and family; about the importance and definition of financial success; and about their ultimate life objectives.

Today, Boomers are sharing the workplace with individuals from three other generations—each of whom were shaped by markedly different teen experiences and, as a result, diverse assumptions about how the world works and what they want from life. These differing assumptions have significant implications for the role that work plays in each generation's lives, what each expects to receive from the work experience, and how each judges the others' actions and performance, fairly or not.

The other three generations sharing today's work world are:

- The Traditionalists, born between 1928 and 1945

- The X'ers (Generation X), born between 1965 and 1980

- The Y's (Generation Y or the Millennials), born after 1980

How your assumptions interact with theirs will influence the options you face and the approaches you choose over the next thirty years.

Let's begin by tracing the evolution of the Boomers' unique outlook on life.

## Boomers

Boomers are defined by most demographers as those born between 1946 and 1964 (see "Boomers"). Originally called "Baby Boomers," demographers have by now dropped the "baby" name. Your teen years, the time when you in all likelihood would have taken your first good look at the world around you and formed your most vivid and lasting impressions of "how things work," were the 1960s and 1970s.

Following a childhood that included the mysterious and disquieting "duck-and-cover" drills of the late 1950s and early 1960s, Boomers' teen years were filled with causes and revolution.[2] The 1960s and 1970s were decades of general unrest and discontent. The United States witnessed the assassinations of many of its most idealistic leaders—John Kennedy, Robert Kennedy, Malcolm X, and Martin Luther King Jr. As Boomers, you experienced the Vietnam War, widespread protests, the Civil Rights movement, and, toward the end of your teen years, Watergate and Nixon's resignation.

| Boomers |
|---|
| **Born:** 1946 to 1964    **Teen years:** 1959 to 1983 |
| **In 2008:** 44 to 62 years old |

The sense of unrest was pervasive in many other parts of the world. The Cultural Revolution was under way in mainland China; there was rioting in France, Germany, and Italy; there was a revolution in Czechoslovakia. Nearly three hundred thousand boat people fled Vietnam.

Not surprisingly, growing up amid these events caused many Boomers to conclude that this was a world that was not working well, a world that needed to change. Many, regardless of political persuasion, concluded that the world did *not* appear headed in the right direction.

Even worse to many Boomers, those in charge didn't appear to be making the right decisions or setting the right course—or necessarily even telling the truth. Many Boomers developed skeptical—even cynical—attitudes toward authority. In a world in which authority figures were suspect—not to be fully trusted—a logical conclusion was that this world required caring individuals to get *personally* involved. Thus, a sense of responsibility to create the necessary change fell to the individual—to each of you.

As a result of these common teenage experiences (although any generalization, of course, misses the uniqueness of individuals), many Boomers tend to harbor a significant seed of anti-authoritarian sentiment even today. You tend to be naturally skeptical of positional leaders. No matter how "buttoned-up" a Boomer employee may seem to be, there's usually an instinct to question and, to some extent, resist hierarchal ideals.

Many Boomers also retain a strong sense of idealism—a commitment to contributing to goals beyond self and family. No matter how dedicated to building a career, paying a mortgage, and rearing children you may have been over the past thirty years, most of you still have a deep desire to make a difference in the world. As a generation, you are committed to ambitious, often intangible, visions for yourself and others. Many Boomers are motivated to do something meaningful.

And you tend to be competitive. When you looked around in your teenage years, the other major thing you saw was . . . lots of other Boomers. You "woke up" in a crowded world—yours was the largest group of peers yet—at a time when much of your immediate world was too small for the size of your generation—for example, for Boomers, high school classes were held in Quonset huts because the existing buildings were too small to accommodate this new bulge of students. You have competed for virtually everything all your lives, from a seat in nursery school to a place on the high school sports team to college admission to your first job. Boomers, as a generation, have learned to value individual achievement and individual recognition. Competition runs deeply through all your assumptions about how the world works.

Based on early experiences, you have related to the workforce in two almost paradoxical ways. On one hand, your competitive streak caused most to jump into the workforce with passion and commitment. To an extent, you have played life's games with abandon, in some cases without questioning the rules, and lived the first half of your lives under the axiom that "whoever has the most toys wins"—only now stopping to inquire about the true value of the prize.

Because of this, you've been enormously hardworking and fantastically productive as a generation. Today you still work longer hours than any other generational cohort (see figure 1-1). You prefer that the world

**FIGURE 1-1**

**Current work pattern**

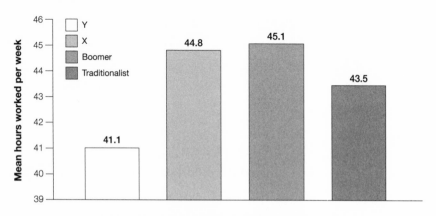

*Source: The New Employee/Employer Equation, The Concours Group and Age Wave, 2004.*

operate on merit-based systems and use both money and position as markers of success. At least as measured by the Traditionalists' rules (by which you've been playing, by and large), your ambition and energy have resulted in great success.

The paradox is that you are also the generation most committed as teens to change—although at least in the corporate world, so far, you really haven't done it. Corporations continue to operate for the most part in ways that are generally consistent with the Traditionalists' views of how the world should work, with only minimal and episodic nods to Boomer values and preferences. You have not yet created business organizations that are well suited to your needs or those of the generations to follow. An interesting question remains—will this be one of the things Boomers put their stamp on during their next life stage—or will substantive organizational change be left to the X'ers and Y's?

Nor have most of you had the discretionary time you'd like to make a change in the broader world. Your passion for meaning is by no means satisfied. Many Boomers today are finding themselves hit hard with a sense of midlife malaise—an "is this all there is?" reflection as the end of the first game draws near and a desire to make a positive difference with their remaining time grows. How will your remaining passions and priorities influence the choices you make for the upcoming decades?

The *Career Curve* and *Life Lure* frameworks outlined in chapter 3 will help you understand your own personal preferences, but the characteristics that many of you share will also influence your options—as well as shape the most successful approaches for pursuing them—since these options differ in many ways from those of the three generations who share the workforce with you.

## Traditionalists

The Traditionalist generation is defined as people born between 1928 and 1945 (see "Traditionalists"). Also known as the WWII generation,

| **Traditionalists** |
|---|
| **Born:** 1928 to 1945    **Teens:** 1941 to 1964 |
| **In 2008:** 63+ years old |

these individuals were born during that war, but were teens in the hustle-bustle postwar years. For many of you Boomers, these were your parents.

The Traditionalists will have a significant influence over your third phase in several ways. First, some of them will continue to share the work-place—they, too, are continuing on to some extent. Perhaps more significantly, this generation shaped many of the policies and procedures that govern how our corporations work today. Understanding the Traditionalists' point of view better will help you see which aspects of corporate life are based on their preferences rather than any operational constraint—and may therefore be prime opportunities for change going forward.

Key world events during the 1940s and 1950s—the Traditionalists' teenage years—included the first manned space flight and the successful resolution of the Cuban Missile Crisis—triumphs for government and those in authority. On the global scene, Israel was formed as the first Jewish state, the Republic of Ireland was formed as an independent nation, and the Organization of African Unity was created. Pan Am introduced the first round-the-world commercial air flight, and the United Kingdom and France become nuclear powers.

Perhaps most significantly, teens in the 1940s and 1950s would have opened their eyes in the midst of an incredible economic boom. It was a time of significant increase in economic prosperity in the United States—people were moving to the suburbs in droves and home ownership was skyrocketing. In just six formative years, between 1950 and 1956, the resident population of all U.S. suburbs increased by 46 percent. By 1970, when members of this generation were young adults, for the first time the majority of the U.S. population lived in suburbs.[3] Housing starts soared, allowing 61 percent of Americans to own their own homes by 1960.[4] At the same time, growth in white-collar jobs was outpacing growth in blue-collar employment for the first time—by the end of their teen years almost half of the Boomer generation's fathers would be white-collar professionals.

And, almost certainly, the talk at every dinner table would have included mention of which family on the block had just acquired the latest consumer convenience, as "keeping up with the Joneses" became a national pastime. Particularly emblematic of the cultural transformation under way, was a family's first TV purchase. In 1946, there were only eight thousand television sets in the entire country. By 1954, just eight years later, 26 million sets reached more than half the population. By 1960, the end of this generation's teen years, the penetration rate had exceeded 80 percent (see figure 1-2).[5]

Unlike Boomers, Traditionalists opened their eyes to a world that probably appeared to most teenagers of the time to be heading in the right direction. Authority figures looked to have things pretty well in hand. Global issues were being resolved in reasonably satisfactory ways, and technology promised an alluring future.

Not surprisingly, many would have seen that world as one filled with endless personal opportunity. For most, economic prosperity was there for the taking; with a good education and hard work, financial success was attainable. An underlying assumption of most Traditionalist teens was that they would become part of the economic upswing that was already in progress. The key was to join, to become part of the existing establishment, and attain the financial rewards that it promised.

There were important nuances to this sense of unlimited optimism, based primarily on degree of access to the promising world. For minority teens in the United States, particularly African Americans, the world of the 1940s and '50s held the same allure—but not the same sense of attainability; the path to personal success was then much less clear.

**FIGURE 1-2**

### Increases in television ownership

*Households with at least one television set*

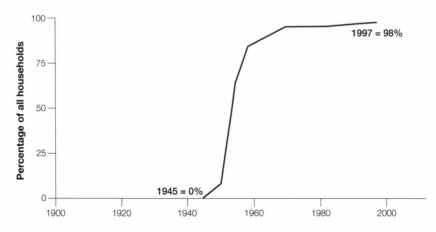

*Source:* Theodore Caplow, Louis Hicks, and Ben J. Wattenberg, *The First Measured Century: An Illustrated Guide to Trends in America, 1900–2000* (Washington, DC: AEI Press, 2001), 101. Reprinted with the permission of the American Enterprise Institute for Public Policy Research, Washington, DC.

Nevertheless, it was logical to *want* to be part of this world: the train was moving out of the station and headed in the right direction. The goal was to get on board and achieve the prosperity promised along the way.

Notice how different the logical conclusions of just these two generations would be. The Traditionalist teens saw a world that was by and large headed in the right direction, led by adults who generally seemed competent. Their understandable conclusion about the world was that they wanted to *join* it. You Boomers, in contrast, saw a world that by and large was *not* headed in the right direction, under the direction of adults who seemed unworthy of trust or admiration. Your conclusion was that you *personally* needed to get involved—and to *change* it.

Unlike Boomers, Traditionalists tend to be respectful of authority and comfortable in hierarchical organizations. They respect structure and assume fairness is provided by rules. They have been the authors of the structures and policies that still govern today's corporations. To Boomers and the generations that follow, the Traditionalists can look rather rule-bound—and reluctant to make major changes in how things have "always" been done.

Traditionalists tend to be strongly influenced by financial reward and the security that it can bring. Most people, of course, appreciate and to some degree are motivated by monetary rewards. For this generation, however, money has a more important, almost symbolic role. It serves as a metric for achievement of the important teenage goal. By achieving financial rewards, Traditionalists affirm—to themselves and others—that they have indeed gotten a slice of success.

Notice the subtle but important difference in the role of money for the two generations. For Traditionalists, money was a symbol that you had successfully joined the club and were reaping the benefits of membership. For Boomers, money tends to be a symbol of competitive success—of winning. Although the significance is slightly different, in the end, money figures as the main work reward and motivation for both generations—something that is much less true for the younger workers coming along today.

Over the next several decades, some Traditionalists will continue to participate in the workplace. Although almost all are or very soon will be of conventional retirement age, many are already choosing to continue working in a variety of ways. Boomers in large part already know how to work effectively with Traditionalists. Going forward, however, as Boomers have a voice in crafting roles for individuals in this generation that involve part-time or reduced responsibilities, it will be important to keep in mind the importance of financial recognition, security, and hierarchy to the Traditionalists. Individuals in this generation are unlikely to be effective and engaged participants in the workforce unless these assumptions about how things are "supposed" to work are acknowledged and, to the extent possible, accommodated.

## Generation X

The generation that follows you—for some of you, your younger siblings; for others, perhaps your older children—has yet again very different characteristics and assumptions. Born between 1965 and 1980, Generation X around the world is much smaller in size than the large population of Boomers it follows (see "Generation X").

This is a critically important generation for Boomers to understand. First, these are the people you will, in all likelihood, ask to take over the positions that you currently hold—and many are not overly eager to step into your role as it is currently configured. Even more importantly, as X'ers assume key leadership roles, whether in business, government, or other institutions, they will have a significant influence over the policies that will affect your life.

Gen X'ers were teens in the 1980s and 1990s—a very different period than the turbulent 1960s and '70s. The world stage was much quieter. The Cold War had ended, the Berlin Wall had fallen, and, as a result, attention was much less focused on global events. The Vietnam War had ended and, although important local conflicts continued throughout the world, their visibility to most teens in the United States, in particular, was relatively slight.

Much of the focus during this generation's teen years was on the domestic scene—both at a country level and, even more significantly,

| Generation X |
| --- |
| **Born:** 1965 to 1980    **Teens:** 1978 to 1999 <br> **In 2008:** 28 to 42 years old |

within the home. Most domestic economies were stagnant. Persistent financial crises flared throughout Latin America. Economic stagnation was prevalent in the economies of Europe and the United States. Americans sported "Whip Inflation Now" buttons, as the economy struggled.

In contrast to the relative quiet of the world stage, the home front for many teens in this generation was undergoing major change. For the first time other than during a war effort, women were entering the workforce in significant numbers. This generation's Boomer mothers represented the first real industrial-age generation of working women, with 80 percent choosing to work outside the home at some point in their lives for reasons other than the extraordinary circumstances of war. On average, the percentage of women in the workforce rose to nearly 60 percent by the time the X'ers were teens, compared with 30 percent when they were younger.

The women who made this step into the external world of work found their entry was, in many cases, hard fought and little supported. There was virtually no infrastructure in place—few day-care centers, no

FIGURE 1-3

**The entry of women into the workforce in the United States**

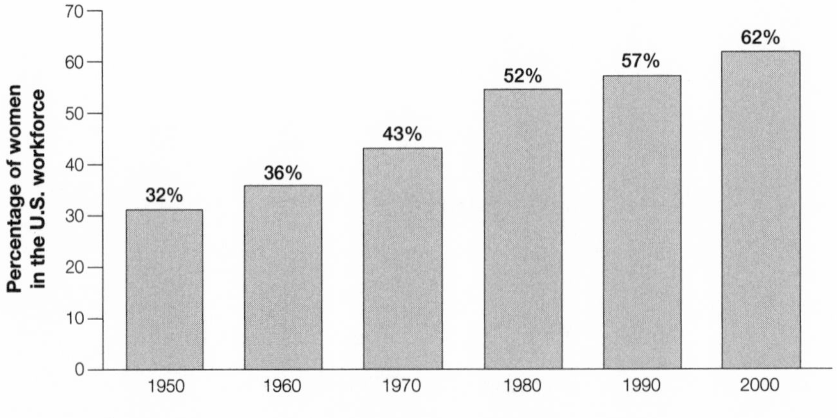

*Source:* Bureau of Labor Statistics, "Women in the Workforce: A Datebook," 2006 ed.

nanny networks or company-sponsored childcare. As a result, the Generation X children became the first "latchkey kids"—home alone many afternoons, often depending on friends for both companionship and support.

The entry of women into the workforce was hastened by the significant increase in divorce rates. Gen X'ers in the United States saw divorce rates among their parents skyrocket from the low 20 percent level when they were young to over 50 percent by the time they were teens (see figure 1-4). The growing number of single-parent homes intensified the likelihood that many X'ers spent their afternoons alone, taking care of themselves or hanging out with friends for support.

Teenage X'ers also witnessed a significant increase in adult unemployment as reengineering and other corporate restructuring dramatically revamped any concept of lifetime employment. It's unlikely that any person growing up in this generational cohort in the United States would not have known some adult who was laid off from a position that

**FIGURE 1-4**

**Growth in divorce rates in the United States**

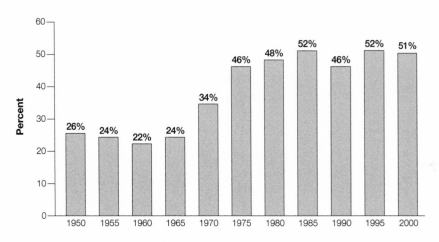

*Source:* National Center for Health Statistics, 2000.

he or she had planned to hold until retirement. It may not have been a parent—perhaps it was a neighbor down the street, or a friend's parent—but the sense that the adults in their lives were being abandoned by corporations that they had depended on for a lifetime commitment is probably the single most widely shared experience of this generation.

The impact of the events surrounding the Generation X teen years is not hard to predict. The need for self-reliance and the ability to take care of oneself is deeply embedded in the assumptions about the world held by many in this cohort. Many rely more on friends for support than they do on institutions and even, in some cases, on family. They are often reluctant to relocate away from their established "tribe." Most continually question whether the job they have today is still the best opportunity possible, and must be "re-recruited" every day. They are uneasy about putting their fate into the hands of a potentially whimsical corporation that could, at any moment, decide to downsize.

Imagine the potential for a generational clash between a Boomer operating under the assumption that winning is in itself an important reward and an X'er deeply committed to a network of friends in the local community and fearful of becoming overly dependent on the corporation. The Boomer's announcement that the X'er had "won" the promotion—to a distant city—is likely to be met with significant reluctance, if not refusal: "It's interesting that you have a great opportunity for me in Topeka, but my 'tribe' is in Chicago; I'd rather change companies than move away from my friends."

As a result, members of Generation X can cause much frustration to Boomers. You are likely to judge the X'er to be less committed, less hardworking than you. Neither competition—a driving desire to get ahead—nor obligation, two cardinal elements of the Boomer psyche, appear to motivate X'ers. To Boomers, X'ers can seem cynical, disloyal, and unwilling to accept challenge and responsibility. This "slacker" image is not deserved; it stems from the X'ers' need to keep as many options open as possible.

And, of course, Generation X grew up alongside the Internet (see figure 1-5). It was in its infancy when they were in theirs, and grew dra-

**FIGURE 1-5**

## Growth in Internet users, 1970–2006

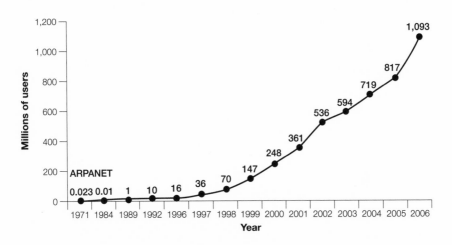

*Source:* The Concours Institute, a member of BSG Alliance, and www.internetworldstats.com, 2007.

matically throughout their teen and early adult years. They learned to use it easily as new capabilities and applications developed. This experience was in major contrast to Boomers' early technology experience—the older of you undoubtedly took your college exams on slide rules! For many Boomers, keeping up with the latest technology has been a continual challenge. Today X'ers are generally comfortable with technology and able to access a wide variety of information. From a corporate perspective, they are unlikely to gain their information on how the company works from a written policy manual; instead, they'll manage their own information flows and communication patterns. As a result, they have caused Boomers to change their managerial style.

Rules have often proved to be a source of Boomer-X'er conflict. The mores of the computer games X'ers played as teens extend to many aspects of life—to them, rules are interesting, certainly worth considering—but if they don't make sense in the specific situation at hand, X'ers are accustomed to changing them. Many X'ers simply can't imagine why anyone wouldn't modify rules that don't make sense, or don't fit the specific situation—for example, by allowing flexible schedules or other reasonable accommodations to individual needs. Holding on to outdated or inapplicable rules for fear of "setting precedents" is a nonsensical concept to many X'ers, who would certainly agree with the old adage that "A foolish consistency is the hobgoblin of little minds" (if they had ever heard it).

This generation expects to be treated individually—to an extent that can strike a Boomer as almost shockingly inappropriate. Imagine a young X'er who shows up for work, having adopted an idiosyncratic appearance—perhaps a shaved head or hair a vibrant shade of orange— running into a Boomer who had devoured *Dress for Success*, that classic Boomer bible for getting ahead, before ever setting foot in the competitive corporate world.[6] The Boomer would be dumbfounded at the X'er's obvious disconnect with the corporate environment. The X'er would be similarly amazed that anyone would confuse appearance and competence.

Generation X as a group has a terrific set of traits—very valuable in our economic society. But to see them, you have to look through X'ers' eyes, not through yours. If you do, you'll see, for example, independence leading to a strong streak of "out-of-the-box" thinking and entrepreneurial energy, tribal behavior enhancing any team-based activity, and lack of a "win at all costs" mentality raising important questions about how we all balance work with commitments beyond the corporation. Working effectively with X'ers going forward requires Boomers to set aside any Boomer-esque perspectives to judge the actions of this key generation fairly.

It's also important for you Boomers to recognize realistically that X'ers are not likely to be your generation's biggest natural fans. To many X'ers, the Boomer generation has been a continual thorn in the side—always holding the vast majority of the "good jobs" and seemingly diminishing the X'ers' limited economic opportunities yet further. As X'ers move into positions of increased authority, resentments related to the results of Boomers' custodial roles—of the environment, say, or national debt—are already beginning to surface. And the workplace that Boomers have managed has not been overly receptive to many X'ers' values and preferences.

As you go forward, striking a respectful truce with X'ers will become an important priority. Without it, there is the possibility of generational conflict—for example, over so-called entitlement benefits (will X'ers really want to pay for Boomers?) and a paucity of talent in the corporations Boomers have dedicated their lives to build. Increasingly, the course in highest demand in many MBA programs today is entrepreneurship; many X'ers are preparing for a work life that does not involve taking on your job.

Repairing relations between these two generations may involve Boomers helping to make corporations more receptive to the needs of Generation X, recognizing the younger cohort's desire for open doors and multiple options, rather than the incessant drive toward specialization that today's corporations often encourage. It may involve getting out of the way gracefully—with Boomers moving perhaps into individual contributor roles within corporations and turning the reins of leadership over to the X'ers. Or, it may involve shifting your Boomer priorities to demonstrate more of the good qualities of your generation—the passion and commitment that marked your teen years. You have the opportunity to use your large numbers in ways that will further agendas that X'ers would support—to be sensitive to their needs as a generation, as well as your own. Mostly, you will need to view their actions through an empathetic lens of their life experience, not yours.

## Generation Y

Generation Y, also often called the Millennial Generation, is beginning to enter the workforce. Born after 1980, the Y's will be the largest consumer and employee group in the history of the United States, some 70 million–plus strong. Y's are, in general, *your* kids—the children of Boomers; many are also the upbeat younger siblings of X'ers (see "Generation Y").

| Generation Y |
| --- |
| **Born:** 1980 to 1995–2000     **Teens:** 1993 to 2014–2019 |
| **In 2008:** 8–13 to 28 years old |

Understanding Y's is important for Boomers. Because they are your children, their fate and preferences will influence the options many of you are willing and able to consider. For all, the large size of this generational cohort means that they will have a significant influence on the world in which we live.

The precise boundaries of this generation are yet to be defined—demographers typically watch the behavior of the generations; when the behavior changes substantially, a new generation is declared; since the Y's are still very young, the endpoint for this generation remains up for debate. Based on previous patterns, however, this generation will probably comprise fifteen to twenty years, including those born in 1995 or perhaps 2000. They have been teens since 1993.

Unthinkable violence has been in the headlines throughout Generation Y's teen years. Beginning with Lockerbie, which occurred before they were teens (in 1988), through the bombings at the World Trade Center, Oklahoma City, and the Atlanta Olympics during the 1990s; the bombing of the Madrid and London subways, respectively, in 2004 and 2005; and of course 9/11, this generation has been engulfed in a world shaped by terrorism. For many Y's, the violent incidents in their schools—Columbine and Virginia Tech in the United States, Beslan in Russia, and, sadly, many more—were even more significant. These events together—unpredictable and inexplicable—have formed an indelible impression in the minds of this generation of how the world works, and shaped their assumptions regarding how they need to live their lives. Eighty-one percent of Y's expect another major terrorist attack to occur in the United States in their lifetime.[7] For many, living life to the fullest—now—has become an important and understandable priority. A sense of impatience and immediacy will be *the* single most salient characteristic defining this generation.

Environmental concerns have also been a prominent feature of the Y's teen experience. Global warming and natural disasters, including hurricanes and tsunamis, have raised their awareness of these issues. Similarly, AIDS and BSE ("mad cow disease"), as well as the threat of Asian bird flu and other deadly pandemics, intensify for any sensible teens today the possibilities of a significant disaster in their lifetime.

This generation's experience with technology has also been quite different—even from that of the X'ers. Generation X grew up alongside the Internet—they learned how to use the Net as its influence spread and new applications were developed. Generation Y woke up and the Internet was *there*—always on. Many booted up long before they climbed onto bikes. They have never known a world that wasn't wired—technology for them is ubiquitous and an essential part of how they operate day-to-day. Y's were the first generation to grow up with computers at home, in a five-hundred-channel TV universe. They are multitaskers with cell phones, text messaging, music downloads, Instant Messaging, and complex gaming. They are totally plugged-in citizens of a worldwide community.

Y's can access information and master increasing complex communal game systems. They have grown up as nonlinear thinkers and are apt to begin tasks at any point—perhaps in the middle. For many, the unique role they've played as the technology authorities at home and in classrooms has left their parents and teachers in awe and added to their sense of confidence. One of their biggest surprises revealed by recent research on Y's who had been in the workplace for only a year or two was how inefficient most corporate processes seem to them, compared with the speed and ease with which they interact with their friends.[8]

If you watch carefully as Y's use technology, you'll see that—unlike the prevalent laments of many Boomers—they are not stressed by it. They have learned to manage it—and its role in their lives—in ways that are helpful and productive, not intrusive or anxiety-producing. Many have clear protocols and *very* explicit simple rules, communicated among their friends, for technology usage: use e-mail only if you must send a document (and don't expect a response); send a text message to coordinate or address an immediate need; share general information, updates, and photos on Facebook; and never leave a phone message (unless it's for someone's parent!). (See "A Y's Signature Block.")

Similarly, many Y's have always had working mothers. Where Generation X's experience was one of change and upheaval—mom going off to work—for Generation Y, mom has always been at work. Generation Y's attitudes toward women working outside the home are both more relaxed and also more *choice*-oriented than any generation before.[9] Boomer women and their predecessors have bequeathed to their daughters an incredible gift—the gift of taking work outside the home for granted. Today's young women don't wonder whether a woman could be the CEO of a major corporation—they know she can and is. They don't wonder whether a woman could be the head of state, an astronaut, secretary of state, or one of the richest and most powerful self-made individuals in America—they know women can and do fill all these roles, and many more. The women of Gen Y are not supporting a cause or joining a fight—they are free to determine the life path that is best for them and their families. The need to prove the abilities of an entire gender does not rest on their shoulders. (Viewed from the perspective of corporations searching for talent, however, women's increasing sense of choice represents a *huge* threat—a major potential drain of talent.[10] It poses the challenge of structuring a work environment that will attract and retain them.)

Finally, Y's have been blessed with an almost cocoon level of parental attention—immersed in a very pro-child culture. Boomer parents, you have loved those little darlings to pieces! There has been a steady and impressive increase in the number of hours that both mothers and fathers

## A Y's Signature Block

*Messages from Y's are likely to specify exactly how you should reply:*

Thanks for your e-mail. To help expedite your inquiry, here's some useful information:

- The fastest way to reach me during working hours (9:30–6:30 Pacific Time) is via IM. I use AOL Instant Messenger (AIM) and the screen name is "XYZ."

- If you have changes to your existing content (takedown request, correction, etc.) please e-mail our production group directly at: hhhh@abc.com.

- If you have a rights issue/dispute, please contact our legal group: yyy@abc.com with the relevant info.

- If you have a release priority (exclusive, prerelease, etc.) that you'd like considered, please be sure to forward advance copies to me along with info (UPC, release date, type of release: new, exclusive, etc.) a minimum of 2–3 weeks prior to anticipated live date. That way I will have time to listen and schedule for you here.

Any other questions? You can always leave me a message via e-mail or phone (ccc-ccc-cccc) and I will get back to you as soon as possible. However, response time with IM is immediate.

Many thanks!

*Source:* Private communication (with contact information disguised) to Linda Stone, founder of Microsoft Research's Virtual Worlds Group and an expert on Y's use of technology, particularly the phenomenon of "continuous partial attention" (2007).

spend with their children each day over the decades since you were children (see figure 1-6). You soaked up the humanistic theories of childhood psychology–permeated counseling, education, and parenting, and have become increasingly involved in your children's lives. Today Y's and their parents share common interests, from movies and music to recreational activities and charitable concerns. The result is a generation of young adults who like and trust the older adults in their lives.

From this unique blend of blessings and tragedies has emerged a generation characterized by impatience, immediacy, heightened social conscious-

FIGURE 1-6

## Increasingly involved parents

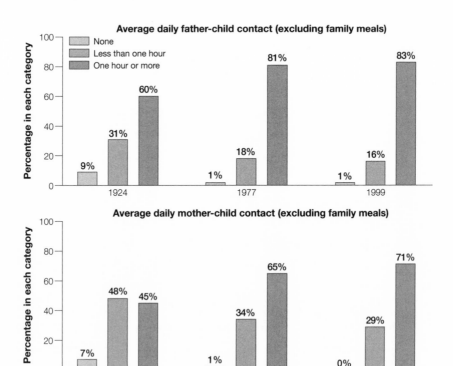

*Source:* Theodore Caplow, Louis Hicks, and Ben J. Wattenberg, *The First Measured Century: An Illustrated Guide to Trends in America, 1900–2000* (Washington, DC: AEI Press, 2001), 89. Reprinted with the permission of the American Enterprise Institute for Public Policy Research, Washington, DC.

ness, strong self-confidence, and a powerful link to their families. Many Y's have been held to higher standards than the adults in their lives have applied to themselves; they're a lot less violent, vulgar, and sexually charged than the movies and books older people are producing for them. Generational experts Strauss and Howe predict that the Y's will emerge as the next "great" generation.[11] The key point for you Boomers to keep in mind as you welcome this talented group into the workforce is that although much of their behavior may appear a bit odd to you—certainly not how you "would have done it at their age"—it is largely a direct result of either your parenting style or the events occurring in the world when they were teens.

For many Boomers, the strongest impression you've formed of your new Generation Y colleagues is that they are *highly* impatient. Probably the most common complaint of Boomer managers working with newly recruited Y's is their unwillingness to "put in their time" before being given major responsibilities. They seem, to many Boomers, to have ridiculous expectations of the level of responsibility that they'll be given and little willingness to pay their dues. And their behavior in the workplace can strike many Boomers as inappropriate. Fearless and blunt, they offer their opinions freely, without regard for corporate hierarchy and with no sense of what would be considered "proper" business protocol—and they expect everyone to be interested in their point of view.

Those of you who are parents hardly have to look further than your own relationship with your children to understand many of the characteristics of Y's in the workplace. Most of you have undoubtedly encouraged your children to speak up and express their opinions. Why would you expect them to relate to other adults, now in corporate settings, any differently? And, how many of you as parents have told your children something along the lines of "you can do anything you set your mind to"? Well, they listened. There should be little surprise that some recruiting officers today report that Y's are applying for jobs for which they have *none* of the specified qualifications—but they have put their mind to it.

Impatience, or a drive for immediacy, is and will continue to be, I predict, the dominant Y characteristic, driven in part by the confidence their Boomer parents have helped to instill, as well as, undoubtedly, the world events they witnessed as teens. They are very eager to live life "now." Should we really be surprised that they approach life with this bias? The need to live life in the moment is completely understandable given the world events of this generation's teenage years.

Ironically, given their generally high levels of self-esteem, Y's interactions with their parents (and vice versa) have triggered a wave of largely incorrect impressions of a generation that is clingy, dependent, and unable to stand on its own. In truth, these negative perceptions are not fair—if you see the world through the Y's eyes. Y's are astonishingly family-centric—and they genuinely *like* their parents. Y's describe their parents as their role models and heroes. Ninety percent of today's teens report being very close to their parents—a sharp contrast to the Boomers. More than 40 percent of Boomers surveyed in 1974 said they'd be better off *without* any parents![12] It is completely misleading to look at the Y's behavior through your Boomer lens—to compare what they are doing now with how you behaved at a similar age—given the extraordinarily different context of family relationships.

The strong, warm bonds you and other adults in their lives have created with them form a connection that is easy for Boomers (who, remember, in general were eager to push their parents out of their lives) to misinterpret as dependence. It is more accurate simply to view it as affection, respect, and a desire to seek out reliable and trusted sources of information. Most members of this cohort are likely to consult with their parents—you—on major decisions, including job selection, behavior that is pretty logical, given the respect and confidence you've engendered. (Now, as to your continued hovering behavior—that's another thing! You must back off a bit.)

There is a near-zero generation gap between members of Generation Y and adults in general, boding well for relationships between Y's and Boomers in the workplace. In fact, Y's are trusting of authority in general, much more so than X'ers or Boomers. Today's teens trust their parents (86 percent), teachers (86 percent), and the police (83 percent).[13]

Money matters to Y's, of course, but time for family, community, recreation, and commitments to the social good are very important to many as well. There is early evidence that Y's may be willing to make trade-offs that Boomers may not have made. Although many Y's are taking high-paying jobs at the moment, most say they are less interested in the financial success that drove their Boomer parents than they are in long-term quality of life. Others are already choosing job options that pay less than other possibilities that might be available to them, but offer more flexibility or family time. They want "good" money—they want "enough"—but they also value a job they love and a pace of life that allows time for other activities.

Generation Y has experienced an unprecedented bull market and economic prosperity and, as a result, has a rosy outlook on the opportunities ahead, reminiscent of their Traditionalist grandparents' views. Coming of age during the most consistently expansive economy in the last thirty years, they tend to have a much more positive, optimistic outlook on life, work, and the future than X'ers did at the same age. Whereas X'ers ran up against a stagnant economy and a tight job market, Y's are likely to find ever-growing demand for their skills. This sense of optimism is allowing Y's to approach work almost with the hope of being paid "volunteers"—joining an organization not because they have to, but because they want to. Psychologically, any notion of jobs for life has been replaced with an expectation of short-term associations. Y's have no expectation that any one place will be a long-term commitment, and they are willing to change frequently as they search the next opportunity that suits them. At any given point in time, fully a third of all Y's are *actively* looking for another job—and most of the rest are open to considering one that comes along![14]

One of Y's important criteria for choosing employers is the company's track record of social and environmental activity. Generation Y is the most socially conscious generation since the 1960s, leading a new wave of volunteerism reminiscent of their Boomer parents' youthful passions. Many are particularly concerned about the environment. Y's support "cause-related" marketing—89 percent say they are willing to switch brands for a good cause if price and quality are equal.[15] And they are spiritually active; 89 percent of Y's say that they believe in God.[16]

Y's will bring a strong sense of collaboration and tolerance into the workplace. They are group-oriented and value building a community. This is the most cross-cultural, cross-creed, and cross-color generation in U.S. history (see figure 1-7). Many Y's are the products of biracial and multicultural marriages. It would be highly unusual to hear a Y use a racial or ethnic term to describe another person; they are as close to being a color-blind generation as we've yet seen. For Y's, diversity including alternative lifestyles is a fact of life.

The bottom line for Boomers welcoming Y's at work is that they are likely to like you—and are generally very happy to work with you, assuming you treat them with respect. Their trust of authority means that they lack the seed of anti-authoritarian resentment that many of you may have felt as young employees. They are in the habit of looking for expertise wherever it's found, and are quick to respect and seek out com-

**FIGURE 1-7**

**Ethnic and racial diversity**

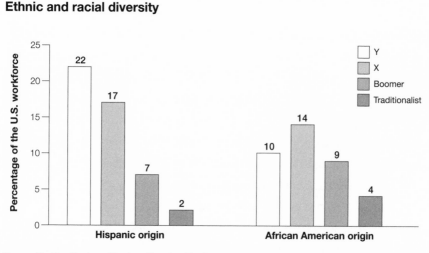

Source: *The New Employee/Employer Equation*, The Concours Group and Age Wave, 2004.

petent Boomers for advice and support. Mentoring relationships between Boomers and Y's are proving successful. One of the most surprising themes of The Concours Institute's recent research on Y's was their concern for their Boomer colleagues; many expressed concern that the experience and knowledge of older colleagues was not being valued by the corporation to the extent deserved.[17]

It seems probable that Y's and Boomers will have the opportunity to team up to advance several shared priorities. Y's already place high priority on the values that many Boomers are now beginning to turn back to—the environment and social change. And Y's will almost certainly push for changes in the work environment much more vigorously than X'ers have had the leverage to do—and many of these changes will also be great for Boomers who are now seeking greater workplace flexibility.

To forge successful work relationships, you, as Boomers, should note that Y's are likely to be more communal than you have been accustomed to being in the workplace (pull in your sharp competitive elbows), and they expect you to share their tolerance of ethnic, racial, gender, sexual, and other personal differences. As I'll discuss in the next chapter, Y's use technology in very different ways—and want you to learn not just how to operate the technology itself, but how to operate in different ways *using* the technology.

From a family perspective, the Y's will have a major impact on your choice of "place" for your next stage of life. The close relationships many parents will continue to enjoy with their adult children, coupled with the increasing ability to work "anywhere, anytime," will support a move back toward families clustering within one geographic location, after several decades of rapid dispersion. Thus, having time to spend with family members will, for both Y's and Boomers, be an important priority over the decades to come.

Of course, any broad characterization of a group omits much of the important detail that makes us each unique. There are many other important bases of segmentation that provide valid insights on other aspects of any individual's particular preferences and inclinations. In particular, there is an important socioeconomic overlay to these generational portraits. However, even with different socioeconomic backgrounds, generational members tend to have similar perceptions of how the world works. Often, where they differ is in terms of their ability to participate fully in the world that they see.

Despite the omission of these important subtleties, I hope you'll find that thinking about the events of each generation's teenage years provides some useful insight into why we each think as we do. "Those other guys" can often appear pretty frustratingly out of sync with our own priorities and preferences—but often their odd behavior looks much more logical when viewed through the lens of their own experience.

*Bottom line:* as you work with people from other generations (as increasingly you will), be sure to think about their formative years for one set of clues about why they may see things differently than you do. Given their different starting points, the differences among the four generations at work today are striking, but often understandable (see "Underlying Assumptions: The World, Work, and Work's Institutions").

## Boomers' Midlife Transition

Many of you today may be finding yourself thinking about the impact or meaning of your life. The values and assumptions shaped within each generation by its teenage experiences have many implications for how people approach work, but they also affect how we handle midlife—that moment when we pause to reflect on our life's progress thus far. This life stage occurs at different times for each individual, triggered perhaps by major birthdays or significant life events. But at some point, most people ask: "Am I on track to meet my youthful goals? Is a mid-course correction in order?"

Against a life goal of changing the world, at midlife, many Boomers are choosing to spend more time in activities away from the corpora-

---

## Underlying Assumptions:
## The World, Work, and Work's Institutions

**Traditionalists:** I want to join the world and benefit accordingly.

**Boomers:** I want to help change the world—but I also must compete to win.

**Generation X:** I can't depend on institutions—I must keep my options open.

**Generation Y:** I must live life now—and work toward long-term shared goals.

---

tion—to increase their volunteer contributions and even pursue alternative careers. For many, engagement with corporate work is declining and a sense of boredom and burnout is setting in, as Boomers pull away—either physically or emotionally—from corporate life.

Bob Morison, Ken Dychtwald, and I have termed this period for Boomers as *middlescence*—a time of liberation and exploration, leading on to even greater adventures—not unlike the period of adolescence that brought you into your first adult phase.[18] Like adolescence, middlescence can be a time of frustration, confusion, and alienation but also a time of self-discovery, new direction, and fresh beginnings. Today, millions of midcareer men and women are wrestling through middlescence—looking for ways to balance job responsibilities, family, and leisure, while hoping to find new meaning in their work. Boomers now must redefine this middle age.

This is the time to tap into your hunger for renewal and launch into new, more productive, more meaningful roles and activities. Most of you would like nothing better than to convert your restlessness into fresh energy.[19] Already the number of Americans working into their fifties, six-ties, seventies, and even eighties is at a record high.[20] The surge will only continue, as the Boomer generation heads toward retirement age, but doesn't plan to retire.

Several studies Ken Dychtwald has recently led continue to dispel the traditional stereotypes of middle age as a time of decline and midlife crisis. In fact, forty- to fifty-nine-year-olds are gearing up, not winding down. You report feeling more successful and less stressed and overwhelmed than younger adults. You also feel more liberated.[21]

Most Boomers have a pretty positive outlook on the years ahead (see figure 1-8). Only 23 percent of you feel that your best years are behind you—76 percent say the best years are ahead. Shockingly, you Boomers are actually three times more optimistic in your outlook than your younger colleagues—you are three times more likely to say that your best years are ahead, compared with younger adults.[22]

Indeed they are. And this book is designed to help you make the most of them.

**FIGURE 1-8**

**Boomers enjoying "middlescence"**

*Boomers are optimistic that the best years are ahead of, not behind, them.*

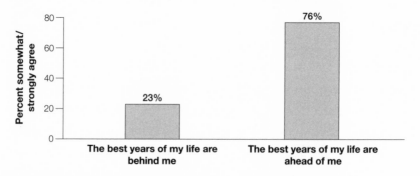

*Source:* Age Wave, Harris Interactive, *TV Land's New Generation Gap Study*, 2006.

CHAPTER TWO

# Challenge Your Assumptions— and Your Employer's

Changes in today's world are expanding the options you and other Boomers face. Your life choices are being transformed in four fundamental and exciting ways:

- *Prolonged economic opportunity:* The shifting demographic trends mean that adults over fifty are finally, for the first time since agrarian days, not just accepted into the world of broadly defined "work" outside the home, but truly needed there. The skills and knowledge you have will be essential to the continuing success of major economies around the world.

- *Increasingly flexible and "people-friendly" ways of working:* The way work gets done and the relationship between "employers" and "employees" (if those terms will even be relevant) are headed for significant transformation. Advances in technology already allow ubiquitous "always on" connections of both people and devices through the flow of data around the world. As corporations evolve, the work opportunities presented will allow greater customization of the individual work experience and have greater appeal to Boomers entering second careers.[1]

- *A life stage your parents and grandparents never experienced:* Dramatic changes in health care and longer life expectancies will grant most of you an unprecedented *new* stretch of time. Boomers will be the first generation in human history to experience a significant period of non-childrearing, healthy, productive adult life. There is no precedent for predicting what the impact of these relatively unencumbered productive years will be. *You* will define that.

- *Positive parent-child relationships and a rebirth of extended families:* The way you have reared your children has been radically different from the way your parents reared you—and will have profound implications for the fabric of social relationships you will enjoy going forward. Although we love to complain about "those kids" never leaving home, in fact they won't—at least not figuratively. Boomers can expect to have warmer and closer relationships with their children and with younger adults in general than they had with their parents, filled with shared interests and common pursuits.

This chapter is about those four changes and the implications they will have for your options for how you spend the rest of your life.

## Prolonged Economic Opportunity

This decade—actually right about now—a seismic shift is occurring in the workforce. Globally, several decades of declining birth rates are catching up with us. For the first time in modern history, the number of jobs created in many global economies is beginning to outstrip the number of people who desire to participate in the workforce—creating not just a temporary imbalance for a year or two, but the very real potential for a sustained, systemic scarcity over decades. When you add a skill set filter over the raw numbers, the potential shortages look even more alarming to corporations in search of talented employees. We're at a tipping point.

## The Numbers Gap

Although most parts of the United States experienced a talent surplus during the first five years of this century—too many qualified people chasing too few jobs—that situation is starting to change. It's possible that you may be in geographic areas or occupations that still have a surplus of available workers. But, going forward, the gap between demand for skilled workers and the available labor pool is expected to widen in industry after industry, region after region, throughout the country.

This is not simply a U.S. phenomenon. While growth in the U.S. working-age population is expected to slow dramatically over the next several decades, Europe's population will actually *decline* in size; the working-age population is expected to grow slowly through the remainder of this decade, then begin a steady reduction over future decades.

These projections are based on three assumptions: one that is known, one that is difficult to predict, and a third that is in your hands. The known assumption is that several decades of dramatically lower birth rates will cause the growth of the working-age population, as currently defined, to be much slower than it has been in the recent past. Comparisons between growth rates for the working-age populations (defined as those between ages sixteen and sixty-four) over the past forty years (1970–2010) and the next forty years (2010–2050), show sharp drops in most countries. In Mexico, for example, the working-age population grew by 200 percent from 1970 to 2010 (see figure 2-1). Going forward, this population will still grow, but by only 20 percent total over the next forty years—a tenfold reduction in the growth rate. In Germany, Japan, Italy, and Russia, the working-age population will decline in size between now and 2050. In the United States, the growth rate will be nearly one-third lower than we have experienced over the past forty years.

**FIGURE 2-1**

## Slower growth in the working-age population

*Percent increase during the forty-year period*

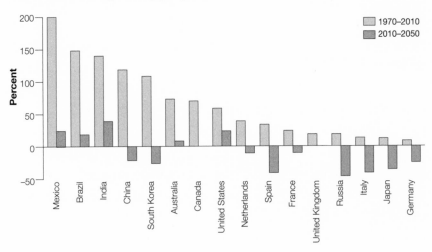

*Source:* Deloitte Research/UN Population Division, "It's 2008: Do You Know Where Your Talent Is? Why Acquisitions and Retention Strategies Don't Work," 2004, p. 6, http://esa.un.org/unpp/.

From 1980 to 2000, the number of people in the twenty-five- to fifty-four age group, historically the prime source of the workforce, increased by 35 million in the United States. From 2000 to 2020, it will likely grow by just 3 million. The current decade alone will see an exodus of 24 million workers, representing 18 percent of the experienced workforce. Of new workers joining the workforce during that time, about 20 percent will be immigrants, many with limited English and few strategic skills.[2]

In Europe, the traditional working-age population (in this case, defined as between fifteen and sixty-four) is expected to decline sharply, from 307 million in 2004 to 255 million in 2050—a decline of 52 million workers.[3]

Underlying this trend is a fundamental change—around most of the world, *we are having far fewer children.* The birth rate in the United States has dropped precipitously, from 3.3 births per two adults in 1960 to 2.0

in 2000—or just about to replacement levels. In many other countries, the birth rate has fallen well below replacement levels: for example, Canada at 1.6, Japan at 1.4, Germany at 1.3, and Italy is at 1.2. If the low birth rate in Italy is left unchecked, there might no longer be an "Italian" culture by 2050—Italy will be a country populated largely by immigrants. Reinforcing that this is a global phenomenon, falling birthrates in Korea mean that the population aged five to fourteen years will decline by nearly 30 percent between 2005 and 2015.[4] India remains one of the few major countries with a growing population, with a birth rate of 3.1 children per couple, still down dramatically from a rate of nearly six children per couple in 1960.

*Bottom line*: the expected growth rates in the working age populations in the United States, Europe, and Japan are all much lower than in the past. The rates of growth in the United States are expected to reach a low of less than half a percent growth per year in the 2020s and 2030s, compared with rates above 1.5 percent per year throughout the 1960s, '70s, and '80s.

The assumption that is difficult to predict is the rate of growth in the world economies, and the associated rate of job creation. However, even with a generous allowance for productivity improvements and recognition that there will undoubtedly be short-term fluctuations, over the next several decades the growth in demand for workers in most industrialized countries will almost certainly outstrip the growth rate in workers within the conventional age band.

The third assumption—the one that is in your hands—is the definition of "working-age population." If Boomers choose to work substantially more—or fewer—years, the size of the workforce would change substantially.

Traditionalists have actually lowered the retirement age; over the last several decades, the effective age of retirement has declined in most countries. In the United States, for example, the retirement age for men has fallen from sixty-seven in 1960 to about sixty-four in 2004. In France, the comparable decline is from sixty-five to fifty-nine. As I'll discuss in the next section, there are many reasons to believe that Boomers will push the retirement ages out. Based on where the growth is, smart employers will want them to do so.

## The Skills Gap

A *serious skill mismatch* will add to the potential for a future workforce crisis. The education and capabilities of new entrants to the workforce are not a good fit for the jobs that corporations are likely to create over the next several decades. Over the next decade, only 30 percent of Americans are expected to hold college degrees when they turn thirty (today, the figure is even lower—26 percent).[5] At the same time, the number of jobs being created based on college-level skills is increasing—some estimate that as many as two-thirds of the new jobs created in the United States over the next decade will be designed for workers with a college education.

Today the U.S. rate of high school graduation is below the average of the thirty countries that make up the Organisation for Economic Cooperation and Development (OECD) (see figure 2-2). Denmark, Finland, Germany, Ireland, Israel, Japan, South Korea, and Norway all have graduation rates equal to or over 90 percent, while the rate in the United States has declined below 80 percent.[6] In some areas of the United States, the rate is even lower. California's overall graduation rate is approximately 71 percent and, within that, the graduation rates for African American and Latino students are 57 percent and 60 percent, respectively, prompting Gary Orfield, director of the Civil Rights Project at Harvard University, to term our large urban school districts "dropout factories."[7] The Los Angeles and Oakland Unified School Districts graduate less than half of their incoming freshmen within four years (some do obtain General Educational Development or GED degrees later in life).[8]

The other important variation in educational patterns in the U.S. is by gender. Participation in formal education in the U.S. today is skewed toward women. Today 58 percent of all college graduates are women, and nearly half of all graduate degrees are earned by women. The number of

**FIGURE 2-2**

## Upper secondary graduation rates, 2004

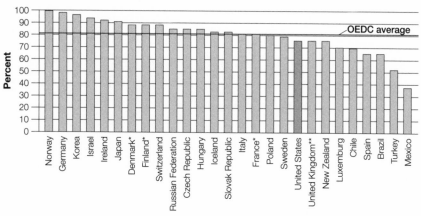

*Year of reference 2003.
**Year of reference 2005.
Source: Education at a Glance © OECD 2006.

women with graduate degrees will grow by 16 percent over the next decade, compared with 1 percent for men.[9] To the extent women opt out of the workforce at higher rates than men, corporations lose a disproportionate percentage of the college-educated workforce.

Adding to the brain drain, many of the most educated, skilled immigrants, including people who have been working at U.S. companies for years, are choosing to return to their home countries. Estimates set the rate of this exodus as high as a thousand highly educated individuals per day. This accelerating trend represents a major threat to the U.S. skill base: more than half of all PhDs working in the United States today are immigrants, as are 45 percent of all physicists, computer scientists, and mathematicians.[10]

These patterns mean that *key skill sets will unquestionably be in critically short supply.* The workforce will not—and in many instances, already does not—have the optimum mix of talent needed by today's increasingly knowledge-intensive industries. The mismatch between skills available and skills in demand is particularly acute in engineering and science, although the shortage is spreading to college-educated individuals in general. We are on the brink of critical shortages in a number of skill areas, again, assuming the Boomers' approach to retirement remains unchanged.

Europe is also facing widening shortages in many key skill sets. In the category of advanced technology skills, the number of unfilled job openings across Europe as a whole is expected to double in just three years, going from 8 percent in 2005 to 16 percent in 2008. In some countries, the sense of being at a tipping point is even more palpable: Spain, for example, is expected to go from a shortage of 7 percent in 2005 to nearly 16 percent in 2008, Germany from 6 percent to 18 percent, and France from 6 percent to 12 percent.[11] In the space of three years, many European countries will experience a rapid increase in the number of job openings that go unfilled as the scarcity of highly qualified talent grows.

Corporations increasingly understand that their future workforce must be drawn from a variety of locations around the world, tapping countries in which the number of workers with needed skills is growing. At the same time, signs of critical shortages in some skill sets are beginning to appear in some of the popular sourcing destinations of the past decade, including India and China. Increasingly, there will be opportunities for those with the strongest skills to compete for jobs on a virtual basis, independent of location (see "This Century's Workforce").

For individuals of any age with strong, up-to-date skills—capabilities that are in demand by the growing information economy—this is all good news.

*Bottom line*: the skills and knowledge that you Boomers have will be essential to the continuing success of major economies around the world. The gap between the number of people who will be available to work and the demand for workers will continue to widen. This forecasted scarcity of talent creates an almost-guaranteed corporate market for your skills and energy—if you decide to be an ongoing member of the workforce.

| This Century's Workforce | |
|---|---|
| Limited availability | Lacking key skills |
| Chronologically older | Global and virtual |

The tightening workforce also presents an important opportunity to rethink the relationship between individuals and "work." This change in the raw numbers brings a shift in power—those of you who want to work in the corporate world will be able to use your new-found leverage to force options for doing so in ways that are quite different from the structured roles you may have experienced to date.

And, if corporate life is no longer for you, the shortage of talent opens a wide set of options for other avenues of productive contribution, whether in entrepreneurial settings, nonprofits, or any other host of organizations that will desperately need your skills and capabilities.

## New Ways of Working

Something big is happening.

The basis of our economy—the way we work—has been changing for centuries, but over time, the "big steps" from pattern to pattern are clear: from a largely agrarian economy to an industrial one; from manual labor to information-based work; from one-on-one sales to mass markets.

Today we clearly are at the vanguard of another big step. The exact outlines and possibilities will continue to be shaped over the next decade, but several dimensions have already emerged: extraordinary advances in the technologies associated with coordination and collaboration are allowing companies to operate in fundamentally different ways—and both workers and customers are responding to the new choices with enthusiasm.

We are moving to what we might call an *individual choice* economy, both in our role as consumers and in our role as participating workers. From a consumer perspective, we are exercising choice in three dramatic and interrelated ways:

- *Collaboration:* Individuals, often unknown to one another, contribute to and draw from common pools of information and experience, and in the process inform and influence one another's choices of products, services, and entertainment, for example, through ratings and recommendations.

- *Co-creation:* Each time we use Google or buy through Amazon, we not only consume a service, but also contribute information that makes the product itself better—information that can then be used to serve us and others even more effectively.

- *Customization:* We've learned to expect to be treated individually (and to be greeted personally when we revisit a favorite Web site). As customers, we expect products, services, and interactions with businesses to be customized for us—because we know they can be.

These same principles of consumer choice will extend to you as a worker. For many of you, for the first time, new options will allow you to find corporate work suited to your changing goals and preferences. Corporations generally have not been particularly well aligned with the values of many individuals in the workforce—and have not been friendly to Boomers planning a second career. Hierarchical structures, rigid job designs, unilateral employment relationships, and cascading decision making are at odds with the idealistic values of the Boomer cohort and the independence of the cohorts that will follow.

Over the next decade, business organizations and employment policies will have to adapt to the needs and values of the changing workforce. Increasing shortages of workers with key skills will motivate even the most traditional companies to change or face the likelihood that their growth will be constrained by a lack of talent. At the core, the relationship between employees and employers—or perhaps more accurately, between workers and the organizers of work—will be redefined. These shifts will both reinforce and enable the desires of individual workers, allowing greater personal flexibility, autonomy, and participation.

By the quarter-century, most corporations will operate as what my colleagues and I have termed *next-generation enterprises*: intensely collaborative, continually informed, technologically adept, and skilled at ongoing experimentation. Rather than operating within rigid boundaries, these organizations will operate as connected communities encompassing a wide variety of partners and contractor relationships. They will tap regional "hot spots" around the world—nodes of connectivity, talent, and infrastructure.[12] Even within one geographic location, work will increasingly be done anywhere, anytime, rather than in fixed locations on 9-to-5 schedules. There will be opportunities for you to offer niche competencies that employers will tap through a network of specialists rather than via today's full-time employee arrangements. Companies will adopt flexible relationships and continual active connections to attract both talented employees and loyal customers.

New technology, much of it available only within the last several years, enables these profound changes by allowing substantially different levels of flexibility, collaboration, and connectivity. Although businesses have been sharing episodic transactional information for several decades, it is increasingly possible to collect, store, and employ nontransactional information (i.e., conversations, wisdom, and know-how). A generation of Internet-related technologies, often referred to as Web 2.0, will, in a sense, cause technology to disappear as a barrier to the execution of virtually any strategy or experimental idea, as corporations become increasingly able to access the information and infrastructure required in minimal time and cost.

The drivers behind this next big step are straightforward: people probably would have always preferred more choice; technology now allows it.

The realities of today's competitive and financial environment increase the pressure to change.

## Implications for the Way You Work

Changes in how corporations operate will prompt changes in the way you work. Your flexibility will grow, and the fundamental nature of the work processes you'll be involved in will evolve as well. The way you work will increasingly be asynchronous, based on coordination, machine-enhanced, collaborative, and alone.

"Time shifting" will come to work. Much more of your work will be done *anytime*—rather than on a fixed schedule—and *asynchronously*—rather than in concert with your work colleagues. The technological forerunners of time shifting are digital recorders—like TiVo—and iPods, both of which allow you to shift away from the broadcast schedules imposed by TV or radio to those of your own design. These technologies have some potentially negative implications—a reduction in the sense of shared experience that watching common television shows might provide, for example, and the absence of water-cooler conversations about last night's episode. But of course they also provide far greater flexibility to shape personalized schedules.

Time-shifting seems to be the almost-inevitable outcome of any opportunity to do so. From the moment a TiVo enters the home, most parents report that their teenagers no longer watch *any* programs at the scheduled broadcast time—they even watch previously recorded shows as new ones are being recorded! Younger workers are already carrying these habits into the workplace, expressing strong preferences to be able to conduct their activities "whenever." And they're pretty amazed at corporate life's rigid schedules: as one young worker in a recent research survey asked, "What is it with you people and 8:30 a.m.?"[13]

Granted, we've been communicating asynchronously for thousands of years—from the drawings on cave walls onward. But new technologies give us far more convenient and powerful ways to do so, reaching many more people. They also allow us to share information with anyone who seeks it and solve problems through communal wisdom. The popular social networking sites like MySpace and Facebook not only allow users to post information that can be read by existing friends at their convenience, but even more interestingly, these sites allow participants to meet new friends who share common interests. Within Facebook there are thousands of subgroups—individuals who may never have met in person, but who share a common interest or hobby, attend the same school, or plan to travel to the same destination. These new subgroups form with lightening speed. For example, since colleges now commonly use e-mail to notify applicants that they have been accepted, the good news reaches almost every admit simultaneously. Within twenty-four hours of learning of their admission, virtually all the lucky new members of the upcoming class at one major university had established Facebook profiles and were eagerly getting acquainted with their new classmates, nearly nine months before they would ever meet face-to-face. Many universities are now allowing Facebook acquaintances to request assignment as roommates. Some of the most forward-thinking executives are already employing these technologies within the workplace to promote rapid communication among broad communities.

Your work in the future will also, in all likelihood, involve much more coordinating and far less planning or scheduling than you have come to know. Generation Y's use of text messaging is an early vanguard of this move toward nearly constant coordination. If you watch Y's on a typical weekend night, you'll see that they rarely plan (no one suggests on Friday that they meet at a particular bar at a specific time on Saturday)—instead, they "coordinate," largely through text messaging. To most parents, these short, virtually content-free messages may seem a ridiculous waste of battery life—after all, what are they really communicating? In fact, what they are doing is coordinating—sharing bites of information about their current momentary location, where they are headed, and when they will arrive. This information allows them to home in on each other like ships using radar. Our recent research on Generation Y's in the corporate workplace found that most feel that they and their friends get things done (arrange meetings, resolve conflicts) much more quickly and easily than conventional corporate work practices allow.[14]

Information technology is not the only force of change in the workplace. Your future work life will also likely leverage robotlike machines to do many tasks that are done by human workers today. Paul Saffo, a renowned explorer of long-term trends and professor at Stanford University, has called machines the "Blanche DuBois of business."[15] Just as Blanche blithely relied on the kindness of strangers, you are probably already relying on the work of machines more than you even realize. Today machines are already toiling away in thousands of applications—we often don't realize they're there until they break. The next big step will be putting them to work in more visible ways that really capitalize on their advantage—as iRobot, maker of the popular Rumba floor cleaners, puts it, performing tasks that are "dull, dirty, and time-consuming so you don't have to."[16] We will soon be surrounded by machines that are able to sense and manipulate things in the environment with dexterous, coordinated movements. Many will also appear to have intent.[17] These machines will substantively change the nature of the tasks left for you to perform.

Within this technology-enhanced environment, you are likely to find yourself working both more collaboratively and, paradoxically, more alone. Gaming technology models this way of operating. Remember when games were viewed as a solo activity—one solitary individual trying to beat the system? Most online games today are in fact a communal activity—collective, fundamentally social—and based on elaborate collaborative skills, although the player is often physically alone.

Over time, corporations and particularly work teams will become more participative—more collaborative. As it becomes both economically and logistically feasible to obtain input from a large number of people, opinion polling—and, in some instances, perhaps even democratic elections—will come into the workplace. This trend will be a huge change for many Boomers, who have by and large lived in a world dominated by individual achievement, competition-based processes, and hierarchical decision making.

Creative processes will be the first to incorporate broad-based collaboration. The rise of so-called open-source approaches to knowledge development (open to individuals outside the organization) allows communities, not just specific individuals, to contribute ideas and knowledge. Recognition of the benefits of involving many individuals in collaborative creation activity—what writer James Surowiecki has termed the *wisdom of crowds*—is growing. Surowiecki points out that "under the right circumstances, groups are remarkably intelligent, and are often smarter than the smartest people in them. . . . Even if most of the people within a group are not especially well-informed or rational, it can still reach a collectively wise decision."[18]

In fact, one of the key points of leverage in business today is finding ways to harness a small quantum of creation from many, many individuals—just as Google does to get "smarter" every time one of us performs a search, or Amazon does when we buy books. These are early vanguards of value creation processes of the future. Marc A. Smith, Microsoft's research sociologist, explained the driver behind this trend: "Whenever a communication medium lowers the costs of solving collective action dilemmas, it becomes possible for more people to pool resources. 'More people pooling resources in new ways' is the history of civilization in . . . [pause] . . . seven words."[19] We are at another inflection point—the cost of collective action is plummeting.

Paul Saffo offers this perspective:

*1900–1950:* The first half of the century was a manufacturing economy. The centerpiece was the worker and the symbol was the time clock. The key question was how industry makes "enough" to satisfy the emerging middle class.

*1950–2000:* The second half of the century was a consumer society and the symbol was the credit card. We knew how to make enough. Workers' power diminished and the consumer rose in importance.

*2000 onward:* Now we are on the cusp of the shift to a third age— the creator economy. The key player is the individual who both creates and consumes simultaneously. Companies that harness the smallest unit of creativity will be the richest.[20]

It is somewhat ironic, then, given the strong movement toward collaboration and crowds, that because of the increasing prevalence of non-office-based working arrangements, many of you will also be working physically alone (although you may be "alone" in a Starbucks, surrounded by dozens of other telecommuters!).

You may even find yourself working in a virtual world at some point in the future. In the online three-dimensional world Second Life, over 7 million people (as of this writing) from around the globe already "live," meet, form relationships, exchange information, and conduct business. Individuals participate, not as themselves, but through their "avatars" (computer representations of who they would like to be). Many "first life" commercial companies have already established a presence in Second Life and need employees—real people willing to man the virtual stores.

## Implications for Your Skills and Choices

Take a deep breath. Yes, working in these new ways means you need to get comfortable with a range of new technologies—in fact, to develop a number of new capabilities. But the changing nature of work also offers a host of new opportunities and a much wider range of choice.

At the most straightforward level, you need to "own" the technology. This is partly a literal requirement: the dividing line between personally owned and corporate owned technology is shifting toward the personal. For young workers entering the workforce today, cell phones and even computers are as much part of their personal inventory as wallets were to you when you first went to work. Soon the concept of corporations supplying computers or cell phones will be as outdated as the clothing allowances of the 1950s or company calculators of the 1970s.

And you need to own the technology figuratively, as well. To be an effective businessperson in the decades ahead, you need to understand not just how the technologies work, but how they cause *you* to work. This is something you probably can't learn intellectually—you have to experience the impact of the technology on how you get things done. You need to learn to use the technology to make your life more convenient—to set limits and manage your time.

Technology proficiency is not the only capability requirement arising from the changing nature of work. For example, as individually crafted work arrangements become the norm, in all likelihood you will need to develop the confidence and skills necessary to negotiate effectively. As it becomes more commonplace for "work" to take the form of contractors and freelancers brought together around specific projects, individuals will need to be adept at making agreements on a frequent, repeated basis.

As you consider *where* to focus your work energies over the next thirty years, look for major opportunities that stem from three sources: changes in the nature of corporations and work itself, opportunities driven by demographic trends, and options based on the exodus of other Boomers and Traditionalists from the active workplace.

First, changes in the nature of work will open new doors for entrepreneurs; smaller, niche-focused firms; businesses built on offering greater personalization or individualization; and business models based on shared or collectively created information. Reduced costs of transactions will drastically reduce the advantage of size. Smaller firms, specialized around core competencies, will proliferate. We may be entering a golden age for the small entrepreneur. Thomas W. Malone, an insightful professor at the Massachusetts Institute of Technology and a visionary voice on networks and collaborative technologies, estimates that the Internet and powerful new off-the-shelf technologies have created an environment in which one out of ten small businesses will succeed, a much higher proportion than that prevailing in the past.[21]

Creating products and services that meet individuals' specific needs will present major business opportunities. In the consumer world, mass-marketing approaches are disappearing—the world of TiVo and podcasts means that fewer and fewer people watch mass-market commercials. Successful businesses based on reaching and serving individual consumers will grow, as will businesses that collect and leverage even small units of knowledge or input from this new "creator-consumer."

A second major source of business opportunities stems directly from shifting demographics. Not surprisingly, given the aging populations around the world, work opportunities in the health-care field will experience major growth. In the United States, six of the top ten fastest-growing occupations this decade are concentrated in health care (see table 2-1).[22]

Even if you don't have the necessary skills today, with thirty more years ahead, you have plenty of time to go to medical or nursing school, if that's what you've always dreamt of doing. Your ability to participate in this fast-growing segment is not limited to the traditional roles of physician or nurse—physician assistants, laboratory technicians, home care workers, dental hygienists, and even ambulance drivers are also in short supply.

Other demographically driven career opportunities include those in leisure industries and financial services, which have grown increasingly prominent as more adults have options to spend time in recreational

**TABLE 2-1**

### The ten industries with the fastest wage and salary employment growth, 2004–2014

|  | % |
| --- | --- |
| Private educational support services | 79 |
| Home health-care services | 70 |
| Software publishers | 68 |
| Management, scientific, and technical consulting | 61 |
| Community care facilities for the elderly | 55 |
| Outpatient care, except mental health and substance abuse | 50 |
| Residential mental health and substance abuse care | 50 |
| Offices of all other health practitioners | 49 |
| Residential mental retardation facilities | 47 |
| Facilities support services | 47 |

*Source:* U.S. Department of Labor Bureau of Labor Statistics. Data from the National Employment Matrix. December 2005.

pursuits and have the need for financial advice. One of my favorite areas of opportunity is in helping Boomers retool around new interests: education, career counseling, entrepreneurial coaching, new venture funding, collectives designed to funnel Boomers' business skills into social contributions, and any other ventures aimed at meeting the challenge of middlescence will be positioned for success over the next several decades.

Third, filling the shoes of retiring Traditionalists and Boomers will be a significant source of work opportunity going forward, even if a field's underlying growth rate does not place it among the fastest-growing segments. The generations have tended to gravitate to different industries, so the retirement of Boomers and Traditionalists will not be spread evenly across the economy (see figure 2-3). In the United States today, Boomers have the highest presence in government service and health care (remember the idealism!), as well as in manufacturing. Traditionalists have the highest concentrations today in education, professional services (probably owing to the number of "retired" executives who are consulting), the nonprofit sector (again, owing to retirees giving back), and, somewhat

**FIGURE 2-3**

**Varying industry concentration: Boomer and Traditionalist preferences**

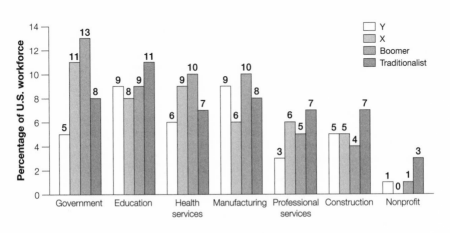

Source: *The New Employee/Employer Equation*, The Concours Group and Age Wave, 2004.

surprisingly, construction. These industries, particularly government service and education, as well as health care, should present good job opportunities in the future. Gen X'ers and Y's are currently concentrated in service industries and retail, with X'ers having the highest presence of all the generations in information technology and Y's in financial services (see figure 2-4).

*Bottom line:* the changing nature of work is likely to offer a number of important benefits to you in your third phase. It will make "work" a fundamentally more attractive proposition. Most obviously, there are likely to be many more flexible arrangements available, including opportunities for location-independent and asynchronous work. Working will become more convenient. In addition, demographic trends and uneven retirement patterns will create significant shortages in key sectors of the economy—and a real need for Boomers' skills to fill them, further strengthening Boomers' ability to negotiate for individually attractive arrangements.

Working virtually will mean that it will be easier to be anonymous—or, more precisely, to be defined by your earned online reputation rather

**FIGURE 2-4**

**Varying industry concentration: Generation X and Y preferences**

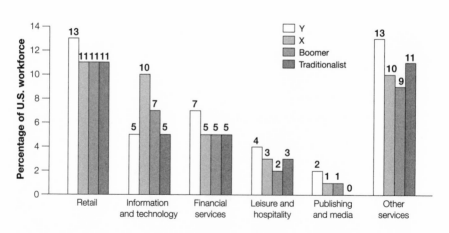

Source: *The New Employee/Employer Equation*, The Concours Group and Age Wave, 2004.

than any physical characteristics. The workplace is therefore likely to be less marked by concerns about ageism or any other form of physical prejudice, and more merit based. The shift to more knowledge-based and fewer physically demanding jobs will also favor older employees.

Perhaps most important, this should be an exciting environment—one you will *want* to join. Business strategies will be based on agile experimentation. Top-down direction and annual strategic planning cycles will be replaced by rapid waves of near-term experimental initiatives brought into focus by a shared view of a company's long-term strategic direction. Growth will emerge from the creativity and innovation that come from a shift in control—top-down to bottom-up—driven by engaged employees, partners, and even customers. As democratic or market-based decision-making processes enter the business world, each of you will have increasing opportunities to shape your world of work in the ways you enjoy most.

## A New Life Stage

This century will usher in a new life stage: for the first time in human history, we will have a significant stage of non-childrearing, productive, adult life. Already today, by the time their children leave home, most adults will have at least twenty, and possibly thirty or more years ahead of active, healthy life. How you Boomers choose to invest this unprecedented pool of energy and capability will have a major impact on national and global productivity in this century.

Life expectancies have shot up over the past century, almost doubling in most countries around the world. When the historians among your great-grandchildren reflect back on your lifetime—the period stretching from the middle of the twentieth century onward—even taking into account the amazing technological advances you will have seen, they are likely to conclude that the single most significant characteristic marking your life will have been its *length*.

Certainly many scholars think so. Business visionary Peter Drucker singled out this change in life expectancies as the most significant trend in the modern world, and went on to say: "In the developed countries, the dominant factor in the next society will be something to which most people are only just beginning to pay attention: the rapid growth in the older population and the rapid shrinking of the younger generation."[23]

In the United States, people born at the turn of the twentieth century lived an average of forty-seven years. People born in 1950 had a life expectancy at birth of sixty-eight years, those born in 2003 can look forward to nearly seventy-eight years of life.[24] For over a century, life expectancy has risen by more than one year every five years. Similarly long life expectancies from birth are found in many other countries (see figure 2-5).

Once children make it past the dangers of childhood illness and accidents, life expectancies increase yet further. Those of you in your late forties and fifties can already reasonably expect to live into your nineties and beyond. From 2010 on, the health-care technology already available, such as cancer treatments, could increase lifespan one year *every*

**FIGURE 2-5**

**Life expectancy at birth by country**

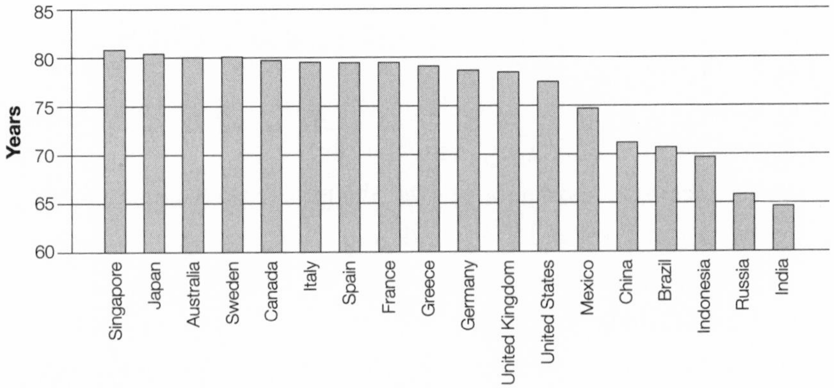

*Source:* U.S. Census Bureau, International Data Base, 2004.

year. By 2030, the average life expectancy in most industrial nations would be one hundred, if all the available technology were applied.[25] Some gerontologists believe many Boomers will have life spans of more than 120 years.[26]

As a consequence of the longer life expectancies, the milestones of life are shifting upward. What is middle age today? The longer life expectancy will most likely *not* prolong your years of being "old"—for most, it will extend your period of an active "middle." Much of this additional time will be spent in good—middle-aged—health.

Meanwhile, in the corporate world, as many corporate leaders are beginning to wake up to the looming crisis of a shortage of skills and talent, they're also beginning to realize that there is a relatively obvious solution to any projected shortage—to tap into the longer life expectancies—to *retire retirement*. For example, some experts have projected a shortage of 8 million workers in the United States by 2014.[27] In that same year, there will be approximately 14 million largely capable adults between the ages of sixty-five and seventy-four, traditionally a group that would not be actively involved in corporate work. If roughly half of these individuals were to continue working, their participation would virtually eliminate any potential gap. Because these people would have the skills and experience that most companies will desperately need, they would not only fill slots, they would also fill specific capability gaps. Even if those workers only worked part-time, they would still significantly close the expected gap in numbers, and greatly help the shortage in key skills.

Contrary to widespread stereotypes, there is very little hard evidence to suggest that a rising share of older workers will hurt a business's competitiveness. In Europe, Danish retailer Netto set up three "oldie" supermarkets where at least half the staff was over fifty, and found absenteeism went down and customer satisfaction went up. British hardware chain B&Q says its "elder worker" stores in Manchester and Exmouth were 18 percent *more* profitable than its regular outlets—due in part to six times less employee turnover and 60 percent less pilfering and breakage.[28]

In the United States, a number of firms have begun to experience the advantages that an older workforce can bring. For example, since the early 1990s, CVS has more than doubled the percentage of its employees over age fifty—from 7 percent to 17 percent.[29] The business results, in terms of lower turnover and higher customer satisfaction, are impressive. Employers on average now rate over-fifty-five workers as being higher than younger workers on key attributes, including loyalty and reliability.[30]

Today, 50 percent of employers say they are concerned about the loss of skills and capabilities that will accompany the looming Boomer retirement.[31] Already job seekers ages fifty and above are getting jobs faster than they used to. In a recent survey, the median job search time for those fifty and older was virtually equal to that of younger job seekers.[32] As a result of growing employer needs and the increasingly positive attitudes toward older workers, the range of options available to those who are reaching conventional retirement age is expanding rapidly.

It makes sense. The traditional idea of retirement as the ultimate reward for a working life loses much of its meaning in today's information- or knowledge-based economy. In an agrarian society, work was part of all stages of life—it was a family affair. Contributions were encouraged by all as long as they were physically possible. Age and wisdom were considered assets. "Retirement," to the extent it occurred at all, was measured in weeks or months, not years.

Industrial society marginalized elders because they had few ways to contribute to it. As jobs moved from farm to factory, speed and strength became a premium and age, a liability. Older workers were unable to keep up. The U.S. government, seeking to ease workers out during the Great Depression, when unemployment levels were above 25 percent nationwide, created Social Security and institutionalized "retirement," based on a concept rooted in the era of Germany's "Iron Chancellor" Otto von Bismarck, who founded the first welfare state in the 1880s. At the time of retirement's initiation in the United States, the average worker toiled in a factory and lived to be fifty. Retirement, for those few lucky enough to reach it, was conceived as a small recompense for physical and mental exhaustion.

The notion of retirement as a vacation at the end of life is a very recent reconceptualization of Bismarck's original intent. In the United States, Social Security benefits increased by 77 percent in1950 and by another 20 percent in 1972, when they also became tied to regular cost-of-living increases. In the second half of the twentieth century, particularly in the 1960s and 1970s, as labor unions gained strength, company pension plans increased substantially, making retirees wealthier. Coupled with greater health, energy, and life expectancy, this greater financial wherewithal created a new concept of retirement as a delightful, decades-long time of pure relaxation and fun.

Today, our information economy provides the opportunity to keep individuals connected, contributing, vital, and productive throughout much longer lives. For most of you, work in some form—paid or not, corporate or entrepreneurial, private or public sector—will play some role in the second half of your life.

Many Boomers, and some Traditionalists, are already planning to work longer. In the United States, already a full third of recently "retired" seniors go on to pursue a second career.[33] In the thirty OECD countries, employment rates for workers fifty-five to sixty-four have risen from 46 percent in 1994 to 51 percent in 2004.[34] Thirty-four percent of all U.S. workers says they plan *never* to retire (see figure 2-6).[35] Among Boomers, three-quarters say they plan to keep working. In Japan, 78 percent of Boomers between the ages of fifty-five and fifty-nine say they plan to work beyond the official retirement age of sixty.[36]

Your decision—whether to work longer and retire later, whether never to retire at all—will, of course, depend on a wide variety of factors. Some of you may have more or less flexibility in making this decision than others. Issues around your financial and physical health are not addressed in detail in this book. However, as you think about how they influence your dreams for your next thirty years, do keep in mind that

**FIGURE 2-6**

## Many employees plan not to retire

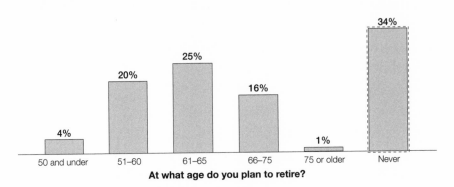

At what age do you plan to retire?

Source: *The New Employee/Employer Equation*, The Concours Group and Age Wave, 2004.

staying active is likely to have a very positive impact on both. For example, since people who retire at sixty-two can easily expect to live another twenty-plus years, each year they postpone retirement reduces their need for retirement savings by roughly 5 percent.[37] As we'll discuss in chapter 4, periodic work throughout these upcoming years can have an even more dramatic impact on reducing your financial requirements.

Many commentators have portrayed the prospect for a longer life with a sense of unease and worry. Will we have enough money? Who will care for us? These concerns fail to focus on a very key fact—that this extended period of middle age will be *unlike* any life stage ever before experienced. All these worries are the sort one might reasonably have if *old age* were suddenly extended by thirty years—but they just don't make sense if what you're extending is middle age!

And there is one very positive distinction between the next phase and the middle age most of you have known so far. For most of you, this new phase will be far freer from responsibility. Boomers are destined to be the first generation in human history to experience a significant period of healthy, adult, *non-childrearing* life! You will have *time*.

Time—that rarest of commodities in most of your lives thus far—is being expanded and redefined. Most Boomers will have more not only in terms of the number of years but, importantly, in the number of hours per day that can be devoted to activities of their own choosing—than any healthy, active group of adults have ever had before. You are likely to have as many years to pursue a second career as you had for your first career. If you leave your first career today at a traditional retirement age, you should anticipate at least thirty more healthy, active years.

Whatever they may choose as individuals, Boomers' decisions as a generation are likely to be quite different from the pattern the Traditionalists followed. Traditionalists tended to view this period primarily as a time to reap the rewards of a life dedicated to work. Most have relied heavily on commitments from institutional and government pension plans as they have wound down, satisfied with past accomplishments.[38]

Boomers are much more likely to view this next phase of life as a time to create new accomplishments. They enter it looking for new careers, perhaps better balance between work and leisure, and, for many, greater spiritual or emotional fulfillment. Most are looking for ways to continue to earn income, even as they rely in part on past contributions to private pension plans. Perhaps most significantly, Boomers are looking forward to a time to deploy the skills they've garnered through life's experiences thus far toward greater good.[39]

If you choose, these next two or three decades of life will offer a time to focus finally on the life goals you had as a teen. Now is the time to think about the relative role work, learning, family, and leisure will play.

You have the opportunity to create—to define—a new life stage. You have time.

## Positive Parent-Child Relationships

You Boomers have done something really astonishing! As a generation, 40 percent of whom as teens in 1974 said they'd be better off without parents, you have developed such extraordinarily positive relationships with your children that they view you—*you!*—as their role models and heroes. Today, 90 percent of teens report being *very* close to their parents. People who were mistrustful of authority have reared a generation of kids who trust authority. This is certainly one of the most amazing differences between parent-child attitudes as any two generations have yet seen.

You've loved them. Y's were raised in a society that placed high value on children. During the 1980s and thereafter, our culture has celebrated children—the frontier of reproductive medicine has been fertility, and celebrities and noncelebrities alike are scouring the world to find orphan children to adopt. (Boomers grew up at a time when the frontier of reproductive medicine was contraception!)

You've spent time with them. There has been a steady and impressive increase in the number of hours that both mothers and fathers spend with their children each day since you were children. Fathers have entered the childrearing equation in a big way. Today, over half of families with children eat dinner together seven days a week.[40]

You've taught them to work well with others. Teamwork, rather than individual competition, is stressed everywhere in today's public schools—team teaching, team grading, collaborative sports, community service, service learning, student juries. Y's want to be effective members of the team—to do what's required of them.

You've built their self-esteem. One recruiting officer told me recently that, despite carefully defined prerequisites for every job posted, fully 50 percent of all Y applicants at her firm fail to meet *even one* of the specified qualifications. Clearly a generation that was reared with the parental mantra that "you can do anything you set your mind to" has listened well! The secure feeling attained by strong parental involvement has given the members of Generation Y confidence that they can accomplish almost anything, and if they don't, they can always get help and support.[41]

And you've protected them. Y's are the most watched-over generation in history. Most have never ridden a bike without a helmet, ridden in a car without a seat belt, or eaten in a cafeteria that serves peanut butter.

They're hovered over to the extent that college administrators are now calling you "helicopter parents." Protected and polished, they are trophy children in every sense of the word.

Most of all, you have developed strong, positive relationships with them. Your children genuinely like you. They highly value family ties and expect to retain close parental bonds even after leaving home. Roughly eight in ten children who live away from home will be able to say they've talked to their parents in the past day. Nearly three in four see their parents at least once a week, and half say they see their parents daily.[42] They speak with Mom or Dad when they have a problem, and most feel that their parents understand them.

There is, of course, the phenomenon of boomerang kids. According to the 2000 census, 4 million people between the ages of twenty-five and thirty-four live with their folks. To the astonishment of Boomers (many of whom, remember, thought they would be better off with no parents), 61 percent of all college seniors today say they expect to move back home after graduation.[43] It's easy for Boomers to judge this trend as evidence of a lack of ambition or competency on the part of their kids; I believe it is more properly viewed as a sign of the close relationships Y's have with their families.

Today, there is a near-zero generation gap between members of Gen Y and their parents. Many Y's say they have very close friendships with their parents and share a number of common interests—including music, movies, and recreational activities. Members of Generation Y typically cite a parent as their role model—rather than the public figures who served as models in years past.[44] Parents and grandparents are popular travel companions for adult travelers who take outdoor vacations such as camping, hiking, and biking. Twenty-two percent of travelers between age eighteen and thirty-four took their parents and/or grandparents on their most recent soft adventure vacation.[45] Many even describe their parents as cool.[46]

You and your children are likely to remain in relatively close physical proximity, drawn together by shared interests and respect. Over the next decade, families are likely to become more contiguous, reversing the trends of dispersion of the last several decades. A number of you may even go into business with your children.[47] For you, "empty nest" is likely to be a less poignant concept than it was for your parents. You may have a bit more time to focus on your personal priorities, but not a complete sense of emptiness.

Parent-child co-purchase decisions are common; one of the hottest trends in housing is the development of multigenerational complexes, designed for Boomers and their X or Y children's budding families. Most members of Generation Y say they are likely to consult with their parents on all major decisions, including jobs.

Unlike the Boomer generation, Gen Y's state clearly that income and status are not the primary values in their lives—they value their family more. A whopping 78 percent of high school students say that "having close family relationships" ranks highest (above money and fame, among other things) in defining success.[48] Many of them are quite likely to have lower standards of living than their parents. Commentators who attribute Y's willingness to take lower-paying jobs in exchange for more time or flexibility only to an expectation of major inheritances are, in my view, inappropriately cynical. For many Y's, what they genuinely want is "enough."

Boomers—here's the thing: you did it! You are, by and large, the parents of these amazing Generation Y's. Their family-centricity and balanced values are a direct result of the way you've chosen to parent. They love you. They want to stay close to you. Like it or not, they will never *really* "leave" you. Just remember . . . you did it.

The closeness between the Boomer and Y generations has multiple implications for how you will spend your next thirty years. Most obviously, if you have children, your relationship with them will probably influence your choice of where you'd like to live—and therefore may influence your choice of work. Even if you don't have children of your own, you will undoubtedly be working with members of Generation Y—and in all probability, will find that a very positive experience. Y's genuinely value expertise, are happy to be mentored, and appear to transfer their affection for their parents to the Boomer generation broadly. There is every reason to believe that your working relationships with Y's will be a positive addition to the possibilities you face in your second career.

## What Do These Trends Mean for You? More Options

Well, here you are: facing not old age, not retirement, but a period of productive time that is potentially as long as the one you've experienced so far—a second career, a third phase. You've already spent about thirty years as an adult—undoubtedly working hard, juggling frantically, and competing to get ahead. For most of you, it probably feels great to think of doing something different—or at least cutting back.

But if you're like many people today, you haven't given a lot of thought to what "different" might mean—how you really want to spend this next stage of life. Many of you may be coasting along on a set of assumptions and stereotypes about your next stage—all of which are predicated on a very different set of conditions than you now face.

Many of you still have ideas of what life will be like in your sixties, seventies, and eighties that are based on the lives your parents led when they were that age—without fully rethinking how different your experience will almost certainly be from theirs. You may have ideas for how to spend your time that include taking a long-desired vacation—a cruise, for example—or tackling a chore there's never been enough time for, perhaps painting the house. These are great ideas . . . they'll take up perhaps a year or so. But what are you going to do after that—with the next twenty-nine years of your life?

Most Boomers have not created a thirty-year plan—not even a thirty-year dream. But if you're like many, chances are good that you do know one thing for sure—you *don't* want to do exactly what you're doing now—or at least not in the way you're currently doing it.

This is the time to move in new directions. Dream on.

## CHAPTER THREE

# Sort Through
# Your Options

I hope you are convinced that past experience will prove a very poor predictor of the future. It just doesn't make sense to pattern your post-sixty years on how you saw your parents' generation spending theirs. Your time will vary from theirs in its duration, in the nature of relationships among generations, and in the opportunities available. You also, in all likelihood, have very different interests and aspirations.

Let's recap:

- Your logical horizon for work is not five or ten more years; it is more likely thirty years.

- Age fifty or sixty is not a time to begin winding down; this is a time for exploring new options.

- Participating in work is very likely to be more comfortable, convenient, and therefore attractive than it has been up to now, since participation is unlikely to require the same conformity to rigid conditions of time and space.

- There are no hordes of youngsters waiting to take your job—and younger workers who may want to may lack the necessary skills.

- Smart companies will not push you out the door if you want to stay, and they will work with you to develop arrangements that suit your lifestyle.

- Younger workers like you and, assuming you treat them with respect, welcome your continued presence and advice.

- Your children are not eager to break their bonds with you—they are likely to be a richly rewarding part of your life ahead and influence your choice of place.

- Choosing where you want to live can continue to be one of your top priorities at this stage in life—without compromising your ability to do the work you love.

- Technology, used wisely, will give you previously unimagined opportunities to form communities with those you enjoy and care about, and to stay in close contact with family, friends, and work.

*Bottom line:* the possibilities you face are substantially different—broader, richer, and more diverse—than the options faced by any previous generation.

How will you sort out what's right for you?

In these wonderful post–"empty nest" and pre–"old age" years you have an unprecedented opportunity for satisfaction, productivity, exploration, and creation—for reinventing yourself, if that's what you'd like to do. You can be entrepreneurial and charitable. You can pursue vocational or professional work, ongoing learning and self-development, spiritual growth, an avocation, recreation and play, relationships with family and friends, and giving back through community and humanitarian work. You can create a portfolio of activities. You have the potential to reinvigorate yourself, and perhaps even to rejuvenate our economy, restructure our organizations, and repair things that are not working well in today's world.

Already people over fifty are remaking themselves at midlife. Your generational peers are leaving worn-out jobs to start their own businesses. They are traveling the world for experiences with like-minded souls. And they are volunteering in greater numbers: nearly half of all Americans age fifty-five and older volunteered at least once in 2005.[1]

Perhaps surprisingly, the possibility of staying in the workforce for another twenty or so years is not—at least not for most Boomers—necessitated by the limitations of the current pension system. Rather, continued work is clearly something that many in this age group want to do—whether "work" means staying in the corporate sector, turning hobbies into paying propositions, or forming second careers that are directed at the social good.

Money, in fact, is only one of the reasons most people give for wanting to work in later years, and is not in most cases the dominant reason. In the United States, having something meaningful or valuable to do with your time and remaining physically active are both equally as important as money. Although the proportions vary by country, research conducted by Ken Dychtwald indicates that individuals over fifty-five around the world share the multiple objectives of work in later life (see figure 3-1).[2]

Changing attitudes to life after fifty-five are beginning to be widely shared. In a survey of one thousand people aged fifty-five and older, Dychtwald found:

- Less than 25 percent described retirement as a time of winding down.

- Retirement is viewed as another promising chapter in life, not an epilogue.

- 75 percent said they will never feel elderly inside.

- 80 percent described themselves as "youthful."

- Average retirees feel seventeen years younger than their actual age!

- Retirement is described as "second beginnings," "a life change," "a fresh start," and a "new chapter."

**FIGURE 3-1**

## Reasons for wanting to work in later years

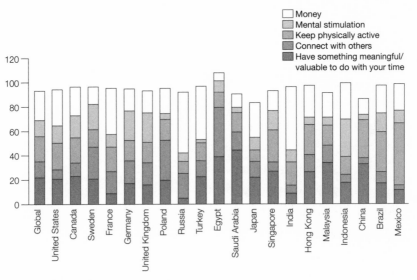

Legend:
- Money
- Mental stimulation
- Keep physically active
- Connect with others
- Have something meaningful/valuable to do with your time

*Source:* "The Future of Retirement Study," HSBC, 2005.

- Retirement is described as seeking "new freedoms" rather than "late security."

- 19 percent report being employed either full-time or part-time or being self-employed.

- 40 percent of retirees have had at least one occupation since retiring.

- 86 percent work just enough to keep themselves busy, challenged, and engaged, but not so much that it infringes on their time.

- Retirees don't work just for money; they work to enhance social connections, learning, and self-image.

- 50 percent said they would work in retirement even if they were paid little or nothing at all.[3]

Are you ready to dream about your next thirty years?

---

## Frameworks for Sorting Your Options

How will you choose among all these emerging, seemingly endless possibilities? What is your career strategy?

Do you want to leverage your existing skills or try something totally new? Do you want to pursue a long-held goal or fill an immediate need? Do you want to stay close to familiar haunts or explore the world? How much time will you want for your family? How much money will you need?

Strategy, in essence, is a choice or a series of choices. For a company, having a strategy implies that its management has a consistent and logical basis for determining where and how to invest the organization's resources—both time and money. The implication for you is no different—to have a career strategy going forward, you will need a basis for choosing where to invest your time, energy, and perhaps money. You will need mental models on which to base your decisions as new opportunities and possibilities arise. Choices, whether made explicitly with data, detailed analysis, and careful thought or made implicitly through inductive reasoning and an intuitive recognition of the "rightness" of a given possibility, are at some level based on the criteria against which you measure each option.

This chapter is about developing your personal decision criteria—a guide to thinking through what is likely to be most important and most appealing to you over the years ahead. Once formed, as you come across various possibilities, as new options present themselves, these frameworks will help you gauge the attractiveness of each.

I'm not suggesting that you gather new data on yourself—strengths assessments or other formal profiling tools have a place, but not in the exploratory process of finding your future path as we're discussing here. Despite the popularity of these tools, research shows that most people make choices about major shifts in life activities implicitly, inductively. Herminia Ibarra writes: "Research on how adults learn shows that the logical sequence—reflect, then act; plan, then implement—is reversed in transformation processes like making a career change. Why? Because the kind of knowledge we need to make change in our lives is tacit, not textbook clear; it is implicit, not explicit; it consists of knowing-in-doing, not just knowing . . . It can be acquired only in the process of making change."[4]

However, as you go through the process of making change in real time, it helps to know yourself well, to be sufficiently in touch with your desires and preferences that you'll be able to recognize appropriate and appealing opportunities *for you* as they unfold.

Two frameworks are powerful determinants of career satisfaction and therefore will be useful guides to your choices. One—the *Career Curve*—is based on the level of intensity with which you would prefer to engage with work. As individuals, you have widely differing views regarding the amount of time and energy you want to devote to work, particularly in these later years. You also vary in terms of the degree of challenge you each want to take on, the commitments you are willing to make, and the economic reality of your need for paid work. I'll show you how to factor these together in thinking about your own personal Career Curve.

The second framework is one that has emerged from my work with corporations and individuals on engagement; that is, the sense of being excited about the work we do, to be so focused that we literally lose track of time. What I and my colleagues have found from our research is that individuals are engaged by very different conditions.[5] Understanding what pulls at your heart and mind, what causes you to feel passionate and proud in the tasks at hand—your *Life Lures*—is very important now. This time you owe it to yourself to choose something that is truly engaging—especially if you didn't in your first career. I'll share research findings in this area and help you think about your own Life Lures.

These frameworks are not the options themselves. They are the filters through which you may choose to view each possibility—to search for options consistent with the Career Curve and Life Lures that work best for you.

## Career Curve: Understanding the Intensity of Work

Over the second half of the twentieth century, employees' relationships with corporate work have tended to follow a very predictable path: most careers began slowly; workers paid their dues with hard work and, often, long hours as they moved step by step up the career hierarchy. Most employees reached their personal pinnacle (or perhaps one step beyond, if you believe in the Peter Principle!) some time in their mid-forties to mid-fifties—their peak of power, prestige, and earning potential. Then, most had a Friday-afternoon retirement party, and—suddenly—found themselves by Monday morning lying in a hammock. Retired!

In today's reality, this makes little sense. This curve doesn't track with our physical or intellectual energy levels; for many it doesn't work financially; and increasingly, it's a huge problem for corporations, which just can't afford to lose major contributors through an abrupt exodus.

Boomers need to lead the way to define new Career Curves. For most of you, this path will probably resemble a bell-shaped-curve. Rather than the cliff-shaped career paths of the past century—individuals on an ever-upward path toward ever-greater "success" until a very sudden end (see figure 3-2)—most twenty-first-century careers are likely to show a career deceleration phase in workers' fifties through eighties that mirrors the career development phase of their twenties through forties (see figure 3-3). After achieving peak levels of responsibility in midcareer, individuals will be able to continue to contribute to businesses in legitimate and respected, although less rigorous, ways. Most individuals today, although they want to continue working in some way, do not want to work as long or as intensely as they have up to now—they want to cut back.

**FIGURE 3-2**

**Traditional retirement: Plummeting from the peak of power and prestige**

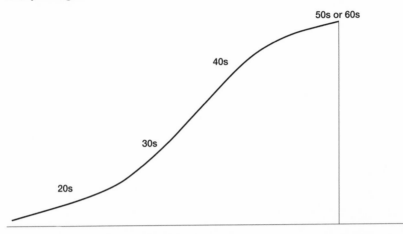

*Source:* Ken Dychtwald, Tamara J. Erickson, and Robert Morison, *Workforce Crisis: How to Beat the Coming Shortage of Skills and Talent* (Boston: Harvard Business School Press, 2006).

Others, however, and perhaps particularly women who have deferred their career ambitions over the past several decades, will want to do more, not less. Some of you see this as your moment (finally) to shine— a second shot at realizing your ambition. If your career has been to some degree on hold because of challenges and responsibilities you've had in other parts of your life, you may be itching with a newfound sense of energy for this new stage. Or, you may have a wholly new dream—a new profession or entrepreneurial goal—that will also tap more, rather than less, energy and time going forward. The bell-shaped curve will not be the path for all Boomers. Your next stage may look more like a series of bells—as one friend pointed out, a carillon (see figure 3-4).[6]

If you think you'd like a "bell-shaped" curve, there are a number of options to consider for what the second half might look like. Some firms are beginning to offer some variation of "phased retirement"—ways to reduce the number of hours worked gradually over time in anticipation of the employee's leaving the organization at some point. Others are

**FIGURE 3-3**

## The shape of careers to come: "Downshifting" for continued contribution

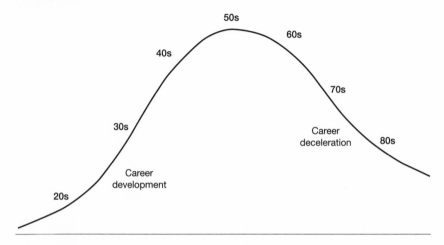

*Source:* Ken Dychtwald, Tamara J. Erickson, and Robert Morison, *Workforce Crisis: How to Beat the Coming Shortage of Skills and Talent* (Boston: Harvard Business School Press, 2006).

**FIGURE 3-4**

## Options for latent ambition: The carillon curve

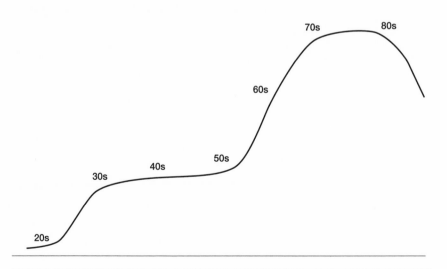

instituting a variety of "flex retirement" options—offering employees ways of staying with the organization, but with reduced commitments of time or responsibility. These may include more flexible work styles, including virtual work options; flexible hours that provide more control over time; or reduced hours, perhaps based on some of the newer models such as job sharing. We'll look at specific options, and ways to negotiate for them, in greater detail in the next part of the book.

If you're not looking to cut back, but rather to rev up, you need to begin to investigate those options, too—and let people know what you're thinking. Many corporations today have essentially erased people over fifty from their development pipeline and succession-plan thinking. The assumption is that individuals in this age cohort are already fully "done," or developed—or have one foot out the door and will not stay with the corporation long enough to return any significant development investment. Of course, given life expectancies, the latter is an absurd premise—a fifty-year-old individual today could have thirty or more years in which to return value to the company—a much longer stretch than any firm should reasonably expect to receive from *any* twenty-two-year-old hired today. If you are interested in taking on more challenges, there is no reason for your company not to develop you for that opportunity—assuming you've continued to hone your own sharp edge. And, although most firms may not recognize it yet today, over the next five years or so, as the talent gap widens, the tragedy of losing individuals seeking to get on a carillon curve will without doubt become more apparent even to the most traditional executives.

As you plan for the next stage of your life, think about the shape of the curve you think (at least at this point) you'd like to follow by considering the trade-offs of time, money, and commitment that you are willing to make. Create your own Career Curve—and hold future opportunities up against it to test for fit.

As you plot your own Career Curve, you should consider:

- *Time:* Amount of time you'd like to devote to work and the role you'd like it to play in the mosaic of your life's other activities

- *Rhythm:* The structure and variety of your ideal work arrangements, including the degree of spontaneity, predictability, and focus

- *Economic reality:* The role that compensation from work needs to play in your personal finances going forward

- *Challenge:* The extent to which you do (or don't) want to take on difficult or challenging roles at this point, including the level of commitment you would be willing to make to learn new skills and capabilities

- *Responsibility:* The degree to which you are willing to take on roles that directly affect others, including assuming the interdependence of managerial tasks

Let's look at each.

## Time

How much time you want to spend at work is probably the most straightforward of all the considerations on the surface, although I will argue that it's also one of the most fungible. To a large extent, the amount of time you choose to devote to various activities, including work, will end up depending on how much you enjoy each one and what your alternatives are.

Nonetheless, it's important to begin reflecting on the overall components of your time. You have many pieces to fit together into a portfolio for the next thirty years: paid work, learning, volunteer work, family, and leisure time. What will you emphasize? What will you do first? When will each element take precedent?

How much time do you have for work?

## Rhythm

A second important consideration, in addition to the *amount* of time, is *how* you'd like that time to be structured—whether in highly predictable or highly variable increments. For example, would working part-time three mornings every week—the same three mornings—be more appealing to you, or would you rather work in episodic bursts? The structure and variety of your ideal life, including the degree of spontaneity, predictability, and focus, are critical determinants of which job will work best for you.

Do you anticipate having other activities in your life that are highly predictable, or are your other priorities more likely to be spontaneous—for example, caring for a grandchild in an emergency or accompanying a spouse on an impromptu trip? What priority would you like to give to work? Do you want to schedule around it or fit it into the spaces between other major priorities?

Most people say they want to work "less time" or "more flexibly"—but there are many variations on what these terms mean. Think about what they mean to you.

## Economic Reality

This is not a book about financial planning—there are plenty of those—but I do want to put some of the downright terrifying predictions many financial experts are making today in perspective. It's easy to combine the extended life expectancies with an "old" definition of retirement years, and conclude that you will need to have massive amounts of money saved and stored up by the time you reach fifty-five or sixty. While of course that would always be nice, it's probably not necessary to the degree you might currently think—if work for pay will play even a modest role in your life going forward.

Projections about the amount you need to have saved by age sixty to carry you through a life expectancy of ninety years generally assume that you will have absolutely no earned income during those last thirty years. What would the calculation look like if you worked at bit during that time?

If your annual income needs after all existing retirement plans is $75,000 per year, you would need to have over $1 million saved prior to retirement, if you don't plan to work at all. However, if you had an annual after-tax income of $25,000 or $50,000, your preretirement savings requirement would be significantly lower (see figure 3-5).

## Challenge

How much do you want to push yourself in your next phase of work? One of my dearest friends, who has held a very respected and intellectually challenging job for the past three decades, is counting the days until she will retire and take a part-time job as a clerk in the pleasant environment of one of her favorite retail stores. She longs for the opportunity to interact with people in ways that will be far less challenging than the first career she has pursued with success. (And she's looking forward to the perquisite of an employee discount on her favorite clothes!)

Others of you may feel quite differently. Early in our research, my colleagues and I met a number of aerospace engineers—some in their eighties—many of whom had been high-level managers at one point in their careers, who were continuing to work—on a part-time basis—on some of the firm's most challenging projects.

How new, how difficult do you want your future work to be? How committed are you to learning new skills?

**FIGURE 3-5**

**Preretirement savings requirements**

|  | A | B | C |
|---|---|---|---|
| Annual living requirements | $75,000 | $75,000 | $75,000 |
| Annual income | 0 | $25,000 | $50,000 |
| Number of years postretirement | 30 | 30 | 30 |
| Interest rate | 6% | 6% | 6% |
| Preretirement savings requirement | **$1,032,000** | **$866,000** | **$344,000** |

## Responsibility

Responsibility is a measure of the interdependence of your work and that of others. Are others counting on you to complete your task in a given time frame? Are they looking to you for leadership or direction?

There's an intriguing trend under way. More and more people are declining the opportunity to move up the corporate ladder. Research conducted over a ten-year period by the Families and Work Institute shows a lessening desire among both men and women in the workforce for jobs involving greater responsibility. In 2002, only a little over half of all men and a little over a third of all women interviewed answered the question "Would you like a job with more responsibility?" affirmatively (see figure 3-6).[7]

This decline in willingness is probably caused by several factors—the X'ers' reluctance to relocate and concern about being pushed further out on a tenuous limb of specialization, the Y's perception that any additional compensation probably isn't worth the trade-off required in additional time, and Boomers' desire to slow down a bit. The bottom line is

**FIGURE 3-6**

**Declining desire for greater responsibility**

*Employees wanting jobs with greater responsibility*

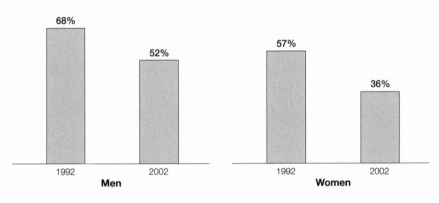

*Source:* Families and Work Institute, *Generation & Gender in the Workplace*, issue brief, American Business Collaboration, 2004.

that this trend, coupled with a growing shortage of talent in general, is creating a dearth of people willing to take on responsibility.

How much managerial responsibility are you willing to assume?

The most likely combinations of Career Curve considerations create several familiar archetypes (see figure 3-7). See if these capture the relationship you'd like to have with work. Better yet, develop your own unique profile.

- *Intellectual:* You like to work in intense bursts, with flexibility and challenge.

- *Customer-facing:* You enjoy interacting with others in roles that are relatively straightforward, well-defined, and service-oriented.

- *Behind the scenes:* You love work that is predictable, clearly scheduled, and could be done on a part-time basis.

- *Interdependent:* You enjoy being in the center of a complex team of people and are willing to assume intense roles.

- *Change agent:* You like to take on significant challenge and have relatively low needs for additional income.

- *Entrepreneur:* You are willing to invest significant amounts of time—and perhaps money—to tackle big challenges.

## Life Lures: What Engages You in Work?

How often are you excited and enthusiastic about what you're doing? Do you ever "lose yourself"—forgetting about time and place—as you do something you truly enjoy? Does this ever happen with your work?

Are you able to resist distractions? Do you routinely invest discretionary effort or produce significantly more than the job requires, often working all kinds of hours to get things done and done right?

FIGURE 3-7

## Career curve: Common archetypes

| | Intellectual | Customer-facing | Behind the scenes | Interdependent | Change agent | Entrepreneur |
|---|---|---|---|---|---|---|
| Time | M-H | L-M | L-M | H | L-H | H+ |
| Rhythm | F | F | P | P | F | F |
| Economic requirements | M-H | L-M | L-M | H | L | L |
| Challenge | H | L | L | H | M-H | H |
| Responsibility | L | L | L | H | M-H | H |
| Possible work options | Project contractor<br><br>Consultant | Retail | Customer service<br><br>Technical support | Managerial | Charitable | Start-up |

H, M, L = High, Medium, Low
F, P = Flexible, Predictable

How often do you find yourself pondering current challenges in odd hours—and enjoying it because the challenge is so inherently interesting, even on the drive home or in the shower! Do you search for ways to improve things rather than just reacting to management's requests or to crises? Do you volunteer for difficult assignments?

Are you emotionally contagious? Do you invite others into your work— encouraging coworkers to high levels of performance and seeking ways to help them? Do you conduct transactions with external constituencies—such as customers—in ways that bring great credit (and business) to the company?

Do you identify proudly with the activity you perform? Are you more likely to stay with the company, be an advocate of the company and its products and services, and contribute to the bottom-line business success?

All of the above are important indicators of *engagement*. Similar to being "in the flow" as described by noted psychologist Mihaly Csikszentmihalyi, engagement is a state of both concentration and enjoyment.[8] A number of studies have shown a strong link between employee engagement and the success of a business. And it's important for your success as well—finding work in which you will be highly engaged should be a powerful goal for your next stage.[9]

If you're like 80 percent of today's workforce, you don't get that great feeling of being engaged very often, if at all. Today, engagement levels are dismally low. Regardless of how it is measured, only about 20 percent of the U.S. workforce has the level of excitement and emotional connection with work that represents engagement. Nearly an equal percentage is actively bitter toward work, with the remaining 60 percent present in body, but rarely engaged in heart and mind (see figure 3-8). In a study of employees from eighteen countries, only 21 percent were emotionally connected and engaged, and therefore willing to go the "extra mile" with discretionary effort (see table 3-1).

Within the U.S. workforce, Traditionalists are most likely to score positively on questions that are typically used to measure employees' engagement with work. They are more likely to say that a good deal of

**FIGURE 3-8**

## Few employees are engaged in work

*Random samples of the working population in the United States over 18 years of age*

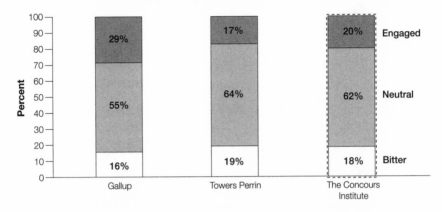

*Source:* The Gallup Organization; Towers Perrin; and The Concours Group and Age Wave, *The New Employee/Employer Equation*, 2004.

their pride comes from their work, that time passes quickly when they're at work, and that they often feel energized by their work. Boomers' responses are only slightly more favorable than X'ers' and Y's (see figure 3-9).

Many of you have probably thought about your satisfaction with your work in the past. But satisfaction does not equal engagement. They're different phenomena from different sources. Satisfaction is about sufficiency—enough pay, adequate benefits, and no major problems or unfair treatment to sour one's attitude toward the employer. Satisfied employees say, "Hey, it's an okay job; I could be doing worse." Engagement is about passion and commitment—the willingness to expend one's discretionary effort to achieve success. For engaged employees, time flies. They identify with the task at hand, their enthusiasm infects others, the activity generates as well as consumes their energy, and they care deeply about the outcome.

Finding work and a work experience that are highly engaging is a very personal quest. What causes people to feel engaged differs signifi-

**TABLE 3-1**

## Engagement levels across the global workforce*

|  | Percent of the workforce | Interpretation |
|---|---|---|
| Engaged | 21% | Connected at all levels, including emotional, providing full discretionary effort |
| Enrolled | 41% | Rationally and motivationally connected, meaning they know what to do and tend to get the work done, but without the emotional connection needed to go the "extra mile" |
| Disenchanted | 30% | Partly disengaged, with dramatically lower levels of emotional connection |
| Disengaged | 8% | Completely disconnected on all levels |

*Based on a survey of 88,612 employees in 18 countries: Belgium, Brazil, Canada, China, France, Germany, Hong Kong, India, Italy, Japan, South Korea, Mexico, Netherlands, Poland, Russia, Spain, Switzerland, United Kingdom, United States. Conducted in May–June 2007.

*Source:* Copyright © Towers Perrin, 2007. Towers Perrin Global Workforce Study: 2007– 2008. Reprinted with permission.

cantly from individual to individual. Some of you care deeply about the social connections and friendships formed. Others care about the opportunity to express themselves creatively. Still others want to make as much money as possible in an as flexible, low-commitment way as possible.

We like to work in very different ways. Some people prefer open-ended tasks, others highly structured tasks. Some like to work on teams, and others, independently. Some need and enjoy a great deal of day-to-day guidance. Others work best when left alone to solve an ambiguous challenge.

We are excited and intrigued by different values and goals. Some people have high tolerance for risk and love the rush of a high-risk, high-reward environment. Others crave the steady dependency of a well-structured, long-term climb up the career ladder.

Four key elements of the work environment deeply affect your engagement with work. Each of these should be part of your reflections as you develop a framework for evaluating opportunities that represent the strongest Life Lure.

FIGURE 3-9

## Measures of engagement by generation

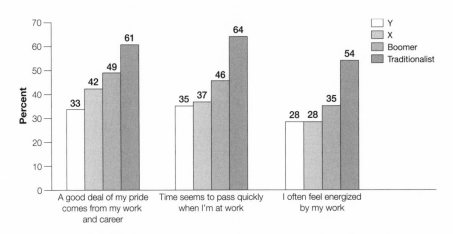

Source: *The New Employee/Employer Equation*, The Concours Group and Age Wave, 2004.

- *Content:* How do you like to work? Do you prefer tasks that are well defined or ambiguous, a pace that is fast or leisurely, a high degree of team interaction or work that is done individually?

- *Compensation:* What do you want—broadly—in return? What is the mix of salary, benefits, deferred compensation, learning opportunities, satisfaction from giving back, pleasure from social networks, or other benefits that you value most from work?

- *Connection:* How do you want to interact with the company? Do you want to be an employee or have a freelance relationship? Would you prefer a lot of management oversight or to work independently? What frequency and formality of feedback do you find most helpful? Do you like a management style that is hierarchical or participative?

- *Communication:* What core values do you want to share with the organization and its leaders?

Organizations differ widely along these important components of the work experience. Some companies have risk-based compensation (options, bonuses), while others have predictable cost-of-living salary structures. Some organizations set up highly flexible, self-scheduling work groups; others take a pretty intense "all hands on deck" approach most of the time. Some reflect an underlying philosophy of paternalism; others a virtually complete contractorlike hands-off attitude. As you think about what you want to do next, it's as important to think about your preferences for these experience factors as it is to consider the actual work you'll be performing. If you don't get this right, no matter how much you intellectually like the idea of what you're working on, you won't be engaged.

My colleagues' and my research has identified six fundamentally different archetypes of people's preferences along these dimensions and their preferred relationship with work. They describe the six roles that work plays in our lives today.

- *Expressive legacy:* Work is about creating something with lasting value.

- *Secure progress:* Work is about upward mobility; a predictable, upward path to success.

- *Individual expertise and team victory:* Work is an opportunity to be a valuable part of a winning team.

- *Risk with reward:* Work is an opportunity for challenge, change, learning, and maybe wealth.

- *Flexible support:* Work is our livelihood but not currently a priority in our lives.

- *Limited obligations:* Work's value is largely its near-term economic gain.

Which do you identify with most closely?

## Expressive Legacy

For individuals in this segment, work is about building something with lasting value. These workers are entrepreneurial, hardworking, creative, well educated, and self-motivated. They consider themselves leaders and like to assume responsibility, frequently reaching senior levels. Many are self-employed or heading their own companies. For them, work is a source of great personal satisfaction. They are the most likely to define success as being true to themselves, and agree that a good deal of their pride comes from their work and careers. They are the most likely of all individuals to say they are impassioned and energized by their work and that time passes quickly on the job. Half say they will never retire. Individuals in this segment tend to place less value on traditional rewards, such as additional compensation, vacation time, or even a better benefits package, than many others do. Instead, they are looking for work that continues to empower and stimulate them, enables them to continue to learn and grow, and has a greater social purpose.

If you share the values of this archetype, judge your future possibilities in terms of the degree to which they offer:

- Individual latitude

- Opportunities to be creative

- Stimulating work

- Opportunities to learn and grow

- Work that will have a lasting impact on someone or something

## Secure Progress

The primary goal for individuals in this segment is upward mobility—a steady, predictable path to success. These individuals are highly reliable and loyal workers who value traditional rewards. They like to work hard and are team players. In return, they want to be fairly rewarded for their efforts through concrete, traditional compensation like good benefits and a solid, predictable retirement package. Members of this group often describe themselves as family men and women, high achievers, and leaders among their peers. They have less interest in "softer" work benefits like stimulating work, enjoyable workplaces, work that is worthwhile to society, or even flexible work arrangements. And they are the least drawn to riskier compensation like stock or bonuses. They seek stable and secure environments and tend to have long tenures with one employer.

If you share the values of this archetype, look for opportunities that offer:

- Fair, predictable rewards

- Concrete compensation, benefits, and a solid retirement package

- Stable, secure work environments

- Work with structure and routine

- Career-related training

## Individual Expertise and Team Victory

Individuals in this segment enjoy work that provides the opportunity to be part of a winning team. They care deeply about being highly competent at the work they do and contributing to the organization's success. They take pride in their work, are willing to put in extra effort, value teamwork, and seek an atmosphere that is cooperative and stimulating. To them, making a contribution is the name of the game. This group is loyal, hardworking, reliable, capable, and typically very experienced. They place less value than most others do on individualistic rewards such as more money or vacation, and express less need for flexible work arrangements. Instead, they place strong emphasis on work that is personally stimulating, work environments that are congenial and fun, colleagues who cooperate, and employers who provide stability and job security.

If you share the values of this archetype, look for opportunities that offer:

- Work that involves teaming with others

- Fun

- Collaboration

- Stable, well-organized, and well-run environments

- Competence

- Work that leverages and builds your existing personal strengths

## Risk with Reward

Individuals in this segment seek lives filled with change and adventure—and see work as one of multiple opportunities to experience a thrill. These individuals tend to be well-educated, successful, and restless. They thrive on exciting work and personal success. They're not afraid to take chances, try new things, and shape the rules to fit their lifestyles. Frequently working for smaller organizations or self-employed, they enjoy assuming positions of responsibility. Growth, opportunity, and variety are what drive them, and they value organizations in which they can work with other bright people and do work that is inherently worthwhile. They own their careers and pioneer new ways of working. They are the most likely to want flexible workplaces and schedules that enable them to work on their own terms and pursue their own interests. Confident in their abilities, they are the most likely to seek out bonus compensation and stock as rewards for their accomplishments. They actively explore their career options and their tenures with employers on average are brief.

If you share the values of this archetype, look for opportunities that offer:

- Opportunities for personal financial upside: bonuses and stock

- Flexible workplaces and schedules based on your own terms

- Opportunities to choose tasks and positions from a wide menu of options and to change tasks frequently

- Open-ended tasks and approaches

- Frequent exposure to other bright people and recognized thought leaders

## Flexible Support

For individuals in this group, work is a source of livelihood but not a primary focus in their lives. These individuals are typically pursuing interests and priorities outside of work and are trying to create balance in their lives—personally, financially, and emotionally. They are looking for employers who can make it a little easier to cope; for example, by offering a flexible menu of benefit options that fit their specific needs. They value employers who offer environments that are more congenial and fun. They tend to view their current challenges as temporary, but for now are seeking new roles and positions at work that will enable them to have control of both their careers and lives.

If you share the values of this archetype, look for opportunities that offer:

- Highly flexible work arrangements, including, to the extent possible, options for self-scheduling

- Generous vacation or options for leave

- Flexible benefit programs, preferably in a cafeteria offering to allow the choice among child care, elder care, and other options based on your specific needs

- Work with well-defined routines—the ability to "plug in" and out again with ease

- Work that can be done virtually and does not require direct personal interaction

- Work environments that are congenial and fun

## Limited Obligations

Some individuals see the value of work largely in terms of near-term economic gain and would prefer work that makes minimal demands on their time. They place high value on traditional compensation and benefits packages, while expressing less interest than other segments in work that is enjoyable, personally stimulating, or worthwhile to society.

If you share the values of this archetype, look for opportunities that offer:

- Low barriers to entry—hiring processes that are quick and easy; jobs that are relatively easy to come by and learn

- Work with well-defined routines

- Traditional compensation and lucrative benefits packages

- Stability and security

- Opportunities for periodic recognition

Individuals clearly want different things from their work experience based on the extent to which they fall into one of these segments. And getting it right—for you—will matter. There is a significant correlation between the extent to which your specific preferences are met and your level of engagement.

The six archetypes from this research are based on understanding the distinct values, traits, and preferences regarding work. Statistically valid, the segments are based on an extensive survey of individuals' psychodemographic characteristics and other drivers of engagement. Each segment reflects distinct work-related preferences along the dimensions of *content, compensation, connection,* and *communication* described earlier. People in each segment care deeply about several aspects of the em-ployee-employer relationship (and very little about others).

Interestingly, while people may shift priorities over the course of their careers, particularly with regard to the need and preference for flexibility (that is, move in and out of the "flexible support" archetype), the research hints that alignment with the other archetypes—that is, many of our core values and preferences—may be consistent over time. For example, the archetypes are closely correlated with career choice—certain occu-pations are much more frequently populated by individuals in one spe-cific segment, indicating that the preference was evident in some form as these individuals made their earliest work-related and probably even edu-cational choices. This hypothesis is consistent with research on the psy-chodemographics of consumer segments; most people do not shift significantly between segments over time.

The archetypes identified in our research have precedent in the work of others on career choices. As noted in the introduction, Edgar Schein initially identified six *career anchors:*[10]

- Technical or functional competence

- General managerial competence

- Autonomy/independence

- Security/stability

- Entrepreneurial creativity

- Pure challenge

He later added two more:

- Lifestyle

- Service/dedication to a cause

Note how closely these parallel the archetypes identified in the research that underpins this book. Schein's description of entrepreneurial creativity is similar to risk and reward; security/stability has many of the characteristics of secure progress; lifestyle correlates to flexible support; and service/dedication to a cause is very like expressive legacy. Schein's pure challenge and competence together reflect the attributes of individual expertise and team victory; and the desires for autonomy/independence are reflected in both the risk and reward and the expressive legacy archetypes.

Most important, Schein's research also finds that anchors do not change significantly over time—once formed, people tend to rely on them. Most career changes wind their way back to settings and activities that allow them to stay anchored in things that they care most deeply about.

Does it matter? In fact, if you look at it through this lens, there is a great deal you can learn about the possibilities that will come your way over the years ahead. Coupled with the Career Curve, which helps sharpen your perceptions of *how* you want to work, looking at opportunities in terms of their Life Lure for you will help you home in on those that most closely match *why* you want to work during this third stage of life.

Imagine that you're considering the possibility of joining three different firms. All three offers are attractive—combining the type of opportunities you've been looking for with competitive compensation packages. They are all positions at the right point on your Career Curve.

You decide to meet with each firm one more time, specifically to talk about what your entry experience might like—what to expect in your first six months on the job. Here's what representatives from the three companies say:

*Company One:* "Your first three months will be a probationary period in which you'll get to know and work closely with your assigned teammates. They'll see how well you work with the group and contribute to its success. At the end of that period, your teammates—your peers—will vote on whether or not you will get to stay in the organization. Management has no influence in the final decision."

*Company Two:* "We can't tell you what your exact role will be—or who you'll be working with. For the first three months, you'll be in our 'fishbowl'—tackling a series of weekly challenges—perhaps designing new products or marketing campaigns—under the close scrutiny of our CEO and other senior executives. At the end of that time, depending on what we observe, we'll help you find the right position for your skills."

*Company Three:* "Your first three months will be spent learning our way of doing business. We have a specific way of operating, and we expect you to follow our processes closely. We're convinced that the ways we've outlined are the most productive and successful. After an extensive training program, you'll get a chance to apprentice with one of our strongest performers."

Which job will *you* take?

If you're like most people, these three ways of starting work at a new company are not equally appealing. In fact, depending on which archetype you identify with most closely—depending on how you view work and the role you want it to play in your life—you'll probably have a distinct preference for one over the others.

If social relationships at work are important to you, if teamwork is something you enjoy and believe you excel at (individual expertise and team victory), the first offer will probably sound pretty good. The entry process certainly drives home the point that this is a company that puts a high priority on team behavior.

If you love the challenge of creating new things and see work as a platform to express yourself—and if you have a high tolerance for ambiguity (risk with reward)—the second company might be for you. Again, the entry process sets a clear tone—intense challenge, high visibility, and chance to show what you can do.

If clarity and definition are important to you—if you want a well-defined path to succeed at work (secure progress)—the third company probably sounds like a dream come true. Clearly they have thought about how to do what they do well—and are prepared to invest significant time and resources in helping you learn the ropes.

Getting it right—finding a company whose values are closest to yours and where the experience of work within the firm matches your personality and preferences—is key to your ultimate enjoyment of the work. In the end, the realistic demands of the job need to be in line with the role you're prepared for work to play in your life. By choosing the company that is best suited to your needs and priorities, the more likely you are to be highly engaged in your work.[11]

As you go forward, look for an organization that fits your preferences and is led by people with these characteristics:

- They excel at expressing what makes the organization unique.

- They know what the organization is good at, and it's not all things to all people.

- They recognize that individuals work for different reasons and accomplish tasks in different ways.

- They demonstrate what they are vividly, with stories of actual practices and events, not through slogans on the wall or laminated values cards on every desk.

Extraordinary engagement lies in the heart—and the key is finding a company (or volunteer organization) that *shares* your core values, priorities, and work environment preferences.

As we begin to look at the specific types of options that are likely to be available to you, keep in mind the two lenses that can help you evaluate how well each one will match you: Career Curve and Life Lures.

Now, on to the options.

CHAPTER FOUR

# Renegotiate Your Deal

## *Getting What You Want*

For some of you, the work you are doing today—the work that has formed the basis of your "first career"—is in itself highly satisfying. You may feel a strong pull of engagement and deep commitment to the skills and expertise you've developed over the past thirty years. As you look ahead, your questions may have less to do with finding something different to do, but rather with moving to a different point on your Career Curve— for some ramping up, or for most, scaling back to have more time for other pursuits.

If this is your situation, the key word is *ask*. Begin today to lay the groundwork to renegotiate your relationship with your current employer or find options that will allow the level of time, rhythm, economic return, challenge, and responsibility that are right for you. If you're not engaged—if this work does not represent your Life Lure—*don't do this*. There are other options out there, as we'll discuss in chapter 5.

Over the next five years, you will see a widening variety of relationships between employers and employees. Many will hardly resemble the twentieth-century version of employment, as more and more companies adopt the characteristics of the next-generation enterprises described in chapter 2.

As new options for engaging with work become more commonplace, Boomers will have increasing opportunities to negotiate for a preferred set of arrangements. Even if it is not obvious that your requests will be accommodated today, you need to think creatively about new ways to work and to negotiate their value with your employer. Be assured—below the corporate surface, there are a growing number of people who are also eager for new approaches and will applaud your initiative.

A lot of people today want to put work in better balance with other elements of their lives. The Y's may be leading the way—many appear to be articulating limits that previous generations have only thought about—but they're not alone. Workers of all ages are increasingly explicit about seeking work relationships with corporations that allow them to retain the degree of control and flexibility required to pursue other activities.

In a recent survey of senior male executives in *Fortune* 500 firms:[1]

- 84 percent said they'd like job options that let them realize their professional aspirations while having more time for things outside work.

- 55 percent said they're willing to sacrifice income for time.

- Half wondered if the sacrifices they'd made for their careers were worth it.

- 73 percent believed it would be possible to restructure senior management jobs in ways that would both increase productivity and make more time available for life outside the office.

- 87 percent believed that companies that enable such changes would have a competitive advantage in attracting talent.

The younger a male executive was, the more likely he was to say he cared about all of this. As these executives gain more influential senior roles, they likely will be open for change.

More and more professional women are making a similar point—voting with their feet: 37 percent leave the workforce at some point. Once they are out, reentry is difficult; although 93 percent want to return to their careers, only 74 percent actually do, and only 40 percent of those return to full-time professional jobs.[2]

And younger employees strongly advocate change. Most Y's are honestly amazed that older workers require so much time to get their work done and are willing to do it within such structured time frames. In general, Y's are happy to do the task required, but can't imagine that it would take them sixty hours; it would take a lot less time if all the face-to-face posturing that Y's view as completely unnecessary were eliminated.[3]

Not long ago, I spoke with the CFO of a major New York–based corporation. Clearly frustrated, he explained that everyone in his department worked sixty hours a week or more—they always had and, as far as he was concerned, they always would. But the company was having no luck recruiting young employees. "Every one says that they're willing to work thirty-five hours a week, maybe forty in a pinch," he complained. "I need you to come in and talk to them."

"Well, I could do that," I responded, "but first, let me talk with you."

## The Inflection Point

Change is on the way. Progressive companies are finding that it's time to get serious about designing a new type of relationship between employees and employers. Recognition of workforce diversity is growing, and most corporations are beginning to acknowledge that few people have "average" needs and preferences. Increasingly, forward-thinking companies understand that the employer's challenge is to create a range of options that recognize individual differences—and allow the work environment to be as attractive and engaging as possible for each individual.[4]

Going forward, employers will give people much more freedom to define what they mean by success in their lives—and to translate that into how much time they're prepared to devote to the job and when and where they're willing to work. There will still be those who love to work so much they never want to leave, or who prefer the clarity of the office to the distractions of working at home. But as companies learn to accommodate a range of time commitments from top talent, organizations will look, as organizational consultant Jon Katzenbach has said, "less like a pyramid and more like a puzzle."[5]

*Bottom line*: companies have little choice—and you have a golden opportunity. To attract and retain talent as slow workforce growth tightens labor markets, organizations will become increasingly willing to handle the variety of employee needs, accommodate employee mobility, and customize more employees' deals. Skilled Boomers looking to create a new pattern of work for the phase ahead can approach the conversations with confidence. If what you want is not available in your organization today, it soon will be, either there or elsewhere.[6]

The current state of practice is admittedly mixed. Many corporations have some form of flex work policies in the books, for example, but employees only rarely take advantage of them. Cultural taboos and prevailing management attitudes dampen employees' willingness to take what is still perceived by many as a career risk.

Happily, however, many companies are beginning to realize that they need to significantly rethink the way they engage with employees—and to create a much wider variety of work arrangements available for employees of all ages. Technology allows it, young workers demand it, women are leaving without it, men are dreaming of it—and chances are, you simply won't stay if it's not available.

## What Can Corporations Offer?

So, where are corporate policies heading? What's likely to be negotiable? What's reasonable to expect?

It's true that after decades of adding deal elements, especially in benefits, in the 1960s and 1970s, employers more recently have been scaling back. For example, currently, the trend in most companies is to shift more benefit-related costs to employees and retirees, as health-care costs climb and retiree pension and health-care liabilities grow.

But the upside of this trend is that it often allows a more explicit give-and-take between employee and employer. With more choice and more responsibility in structuring their individual deals, employees who become more informed "consumers" are in better positions to negotiate specific deal elements. So, although some elements may no longer be available, the deal as a whole opens up new options, especially in the area of life balance. The entire deal—work arrangements, learning opportunities, compensation, and benefits—is in play, customizable as never before.[7]

The philosophy behind human resource policies—those governing the relationship between employees and employers—is changing (granted, slowly in many organizations). For the past half century, the dominant drumbeat has had corporations marching steadily toward greater and greater "equality"—in most instances, defined as uniformity of practice. For many good and logical reasons (initially a desire to create a standard industrial work model, followed by a growing fear of legal action), companies have bent over backward to offer or appear to offer everyone the exact same deal.

The limitations of this approach are now becoming clear. Standardization makes much less sense for the knowledge-work jobs that increasingly dominate today's economy. In addition, as the workforce becomes increasingly diverse, it's clear that different people want different things from work—they get excited about different things, passionate in different ways, and need different types of relationships with the institutions with whom they collaborate. And, at the most obvious level, many companies are offering all employees a range of features, any one of which many individuals care nothing about.

Innovative deals of all varieties are on the horizon. Consumerism is finding the workforce. Companies are realizing that, just as the purchasers of their products and services want more and more variety, more and more customization, these same individuals are in fact also their employees—and they want the same degree of variation in their work arrangements—time, place, role, pace of progression, intensity of learning, and many other variables.

Options around time and place are probably the most advanced today. Employers are learning how to validate opportunities for flex work and how to structure it so that it meets their business goals and employees' needs. Which is a good thing: on an overwhelming basis, people over fifty-five favor flexible working arrangements as they shape plans for balancing work, leisure, and money-earning activities in later years (see figure 4-1).

Already, many of you have some form of nontraditional work arrangement; 43 percent of U.S. employees—up from 29 percent in 1992—

**FIGURE 4-1**

### Views of the ideal plan for balancing work, leisure, and money in later years

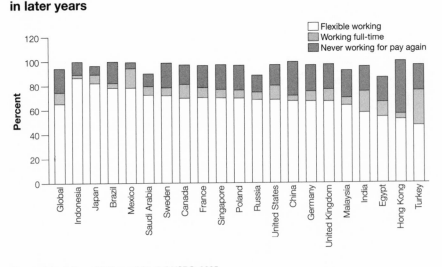

Source: "The Future of Retirement Study," HSBC, 2005.

now use conventional flextime, in which they select their own starting and quitting times around a core of regular working hours. Most agree, however, that this represents a small step toward true flexibility, since once chosen, the hours typically remain rather rigid. Nearly 80 percent of employees say they would like to have *more* flexible work options.[8]

One of the main issues that many companies still get stuck on is the fit between bell-shaped Career Curves and their traditional compensation and pension systems. But if an employer is still at this stage, there's reason to expect that the situation will change over the next several years. To get around the drawbacks of pay systems that reward workers based on seniority rather than performance, more and more companies are introducing "peak wage" contracts that gradually reduce the pay of employees past the age of fifty-five or sixty, often in conjunction with reduced working hours.

Over the next decade, a wide range of variations in how workers connect with the organizers of work will become increasingly commonplace. You should begin to think about your next phase of work with the expectation that the options you seek are either now or could be available.

As you look forward, think outside the box. Consider these questions:

- Are there roles in the company that you'd enjoy taking on that others might be less eager to do? Roles that require relocation, for example, are increasingly unpopular with leaders in their thirties and early forties. Is this something you might like to do?

- Are there places in the world where you'd love to live for a period of time? Cultures you'd like to experience and learn more about? Again, perhaps ones that would be less attractive to younger workers currently raising a family?

- Are you eager to continue up the leadership path, perhaps at a faster (or slower) pace than the normal speed of career progression? What investments in learning are you willing to make to prepare?

- How much responsibility are you willing to assume? As discussed in chapter 2, there has been a clear trend across the last decade of employees answering the question "Would you like a job with more responsibility?" in the negative. The search for tomorrow's leaders will be significantly affected by this trend. Going forward, corporations will have to choose tomorrow's executives from a smaller pool, perhaps with mismatched skills—and will find that many people won't want the job even if it's offered to them! If you're willing, let the corporation know—and what you'd like in return.

- Can you offer to put in odd hours that younger workers with family obligations might not be able to work?

- What are the "high-impact" roles within the company in which your knowledge and experience will make the biggest difference?

- Is it possible to structure your responsibilities so that they are shared among a team of people, relieving the crunch that might otherwise fall on one person's shoulders and allowing greater flexibility to swap based on individual needs?

- Are there roles you could fill that would allow you to work full tilt for nine months and then take off three?

- To what extent are you willing to trade income for time?

- If you have sufficient cash flow, could you arrange to work for benefits only? One of the most important deal elements for most Americans working past age fifty-five is coverage for catastrophic health care (see figure 4-2). I've encountered examples of people who are working part-time in exchange for this benefit alone.

- What do you really want to learn, and how could the corporation help you gain that knowledge?

- Are there options to access more education based on the old barter method? For example, are there training courses that the

**FIGURE 4-2**

## The unpredictable cost of illness is by far Boomers' biggest fear

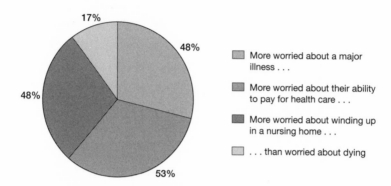

More worried about a major illness . . .

More worried about their ability to pay for health care . . .

More worried about winding up in a nursing home . . .

. . . than worried about dying

*Source:* Shannon O'Brien, *How Baby Boomers Will Change Retirement*, http://seniorliving.about.com/od/retirement/newboomerretire.htm, August 2006.

company offers that you'd like to attend? Could you work a part-time schedule in exchange?

Find out what options your company already offers. If they don't include the ones you'd prefer, begin today to encourage the creation of a wider variety of work arrangements that will allow people to work with your organization in multiple ways. (My coauthors and I discussed many of these types of arrangements in our book *Workforce Crisis*—give the executives in your firm a copy!)

What types of arrangements are already reasonable to expect? We'll look at six major themes related to variations in time, place, and/or role that are becoming available today:

- Flexible time

- Reduced time

- Cyclic time

- Flexible place

- Task, not time

- Decelerating roles

After reviewing these possibilities, we'll explore one other critically important element of any arrangements you make in depth: how the corporation will support you in continuing to learn and develop additional capabilities.

## Flexible Time

Many companies today offer varieties of *flexible time*, including flexible hours and shifts and compressed workweeks. Typical flexible work options include:

- *Flexible shift:* Work schedules that permit flexible starting and quitting times within limits set by management

- *Compressed workweek:* A workweek compressed into fewer than five days; for example, a forty-hour workweek compressed into four ten-hour days instead of the usual five eight-hour days

- *Individualized work schedule:* Fixed workdays with agreed-upon schedules varying from two hours before to two hours after normal location operating times

The most progressive forms of flexible time involve day-to-day or week-to-week flexibility.

## Reduced Time

*Reduced time* includes part-time work, job sharing, and leaves of absence:

- *Part-time reduced work schedule:* A regular employee with a reduced work schedule

- *Job sharing:* Work for which people (typically two) share responsibilities of one full-time (typically salaried) position (see "Two for One: Job Sharing")

---

## Two for One: Job Sharing

At Fleet Bank in Boston, Cynthia Cunningham and Shelley Murray shared the job of vice president for global markets foreign exchange for six years. Each worked three days a week on a trading desk. They didn't divide clients and tasks; whoever was present dealt with whatever came up. They had one set of goals and one performance review, and they operated so seamlessly—with the help of a weekly meeting and constant voice mails throughout the day—that out-of-town colleagues often didn't know there were two of them. In previous jobs each had worked fifty to sixty hours a week; in their shared role they dropped to twenty to twenty-five each. They also felt "totally on" at the office, since work wasn't consuming their lives. The gratitude factor, too, was huge: having a rare senior job-share doubled their drive to deliver. "We didn't have time to waste," says Cunningham, "We had to succeed so that we could keep the arrangement we had."

*Source:* Jody Miller and Matt Miller, "Get A Life! Ditching the 24/7 Culture," *Fortune*, November 16, 2005.

---

- *Leave-of-absence programs:* Options for taking unpaid leave either on a day-to-day basis or for an extended time

One variation of the reduced time option that is growing in popularity is group-based job sharing, including self-scheduling. In shared jobs and self-scheduling groups, individuals find real flexibility when they can be part of small teams or pairs and manage the ups and downs of their day-to-day work. JetBlue's airline reservation system is perhaps best known for pioneering this approach, based on very sophisticated use of technology.

## Cyclic Time

*Cyclic work* is working on an episodic basis. Over the next several decades, there will be a rapid increase in the number of people who work in cyclical or project-based arrangements—many with no fixed affiliation to one corporation. Already, nearly half—49 percent—of U.S. workers who plan to work during traditional retirement years say that they would *prefer* cyclical arrangements—periods of full-time work (say several months) interspersed with periods of no work (several months or more) (see figure 4-3).

This cyclic pattern would allows individuals to work hard for a period of time (with one employer) then move on to another work period, typically with a new employer, or a period of leisure, learning, or another pursuit (see "Greater Flexibility Through Freelance Arrangements"). Conventional part-time arrangements, working part of a day or part of a week, are popular, too—39 percent like this idea—but less so than cyclic, which allows more time and flexibility for other pursuits.

**FIGURE 4-3**

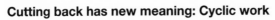

**Cutting back has new meaning: Cyclic work**

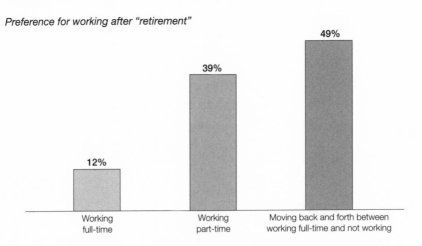

*Preference for working after "retirement"*

| | | |
|---|---|---|
| 12% | 39% | 49% |
| Working full-time | Working part-time | Moving back and forth between working full-time and not working |

*Source: The New Employee/Employer Equation, The Concours Group and Age Wave, 2004.*

Some even argue that project-based work will become the norm—each company having a core of full-time employees, supplemented through a broad network of alliances—with most workers assembled by project, as needed. Consider the film industry. In the days of Marilyn Monroe and Humphrey Bogart, actors (as well as directors, cameramen, and all others required to produce a moving picture) were *employees* of the studio. Today that is far from the case. Studios have become, in essence, financing and distribution vehicles for project-based endeavors—the producer (also often independent) assembling a unique cast and crew for each film. It is likely that some form of this model will come to many of our industries over the next decade or two.

Like many of these important trends, the popularity of cyclic work is by no means a U.S. phenomenon—although it is not universally preferred. While workers in a number of countries, including Brazil, France, and Japan, have an even stronger preference for cyclic work than is found in the United States, those in several other countries, particularly the United Kingdom and India, are markedly less enthusiastic (see figure 4-4).[9]

**FIGURE 4-4**

### Cyclic work: Popular around the world

*Percent who think that going back and forth between periods of work and periods of leisure is the ideal plan*

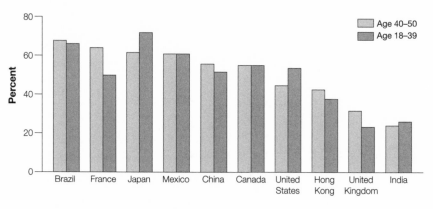

*Source:* "The Future of Retirement Study," HSBC, 2005, 6.

## Greater Flexibility Through Freelance Arrangements

An unexpected turn of events made career nurse Anne Turner rethink her retirement plans. Anne had put in many years as a pediatric nurse, working long shifts in stressful conditions. She had always planned to enjoy a full and immediate retirement until her husband passed away when she was sixty-two. Faced with financial concerns that she never anticipated, Anne knew that she would have to return to work. She also knew that she didn't want to return to the demands and stresses of the nursing career she had left behind. Anne is now freelancing with a private health care company, performing contractual work for home-bound patients whom she chooses, working hours that she prefers. The income, coupled with the flexibility she has in making her own schedule, has made the transition back out of retirement much easier.

*Source:* Joanne Murray, "Make a Late-Career Change," http://management.monster.com/articles/leveraging.

## Flexible Place

*Flexible place* includes telecommuting (working primarily from home) and mobile work (such as a salesperson who works predominantly on the road), and other forms of off-site work:

- *Mobile work:* Working on the move and without a dedicated company work space

- *Telecommuting:* Working regularly at home and without a dedicated company work space

Today, almost three-quarters of the U.S. workforce still work at a fixed location. Only 9 percent of employees work at least part of the time at home rather than in the office. However, the percent working from home—or from local coffee shops—will grow over the century as a confluence of technological enablement, employee preference, and corporate cost pressures drive organizations to seek ways to shift away from bricks and mortar and associated overhead. Support for teleworking has also grown as companies recognize the need for a backup in the event of a natural disaster or terror attack.[10] Thus the rootless army—the so-called "Kinko's Club" (employees who spend significant hours each month working outside of a traditional office)—is growing by 10 percent annually.[11]

Working from home or other virtual locations allows those who are comfortable doing so to work anytime, anywhere. When workers can arrange their schedules to be on the job during their most productive times—and avoid prolonged and unproductive commutes—productivity rises. In a survey of fifty-nine thousand people in forty-eight countries, employees who worked at home rated themselves as more productive than workers in any other work arrangement category.[12] A company can save significant direct cost in real estate and facilities when employees work primarily off-site. Consumption of personal and sick days and attendant costs decline when employees have more flexibility to attend to personal concerns in the day-to-day flow of their jobs.

## Task, Not Time

One of the most exciting options looming on the work horizon is the concept of switching to "task-based" rather than "time-based" work arrangements. The essence of this approach is to assign employees specific tasks and require them to put in only as much time as it actually takes to get the work done. Following this to its logical end removes restrictions and expectations within which corporate workers traditionally labor—such as keeping regular hours and showing up at the office each morning.

Structuring work in this way allows people to work asynchronously—instead of in standard 9-to-5 routines and virtually from any location. These approaches will fit well with the preferences of Generation Y, but will also be powerful aids to the blended lifestyles many Boomers are looking for in the years ahead.

Best Buy is one company that has been moving to a "task, not time" environment over the last several years. In what it calls a "Results-Only Work Environment," or ROWE, employees are allowed to decide how, when, and where they get the job done. Whether they choose to work in the office, at home, or somewhere else, salaried employees are required to put in only as much time as it actually takes to do their work. (Hourly employees in the program have to work a set number of hours to comply with federal labor regulations, but they still get to choose when they do it.) Physical attendance at meetings is usually optional. As for supervisors, the only yardstick for evaluating employees is whether they meet goals for productivity.[13]

Sounds great—but not like anything you could achieve at your firm? Well, don't give up hope.

ROWE has had a significant positive impact at Best Buy. Employees report that they have better relationships with family and friends, feel more loyalty to the company, and feel more focused and energized about their work. And from a business standpoint, there are financial benefits. ROWE teams have less voluntary turnover than non-ROWE teams and higher productivity.

In designing the system, Best Buy's leaders considered more conventional flextime and telecommuting options, but concluded they didn't go far enough. Concerns with conventional flextime approaches included:

- The possibility of favoritism exists if managers choose to give flexibility to a few select people. ROWE gives it to the whole department at once; no one can be turned down and nobody has to ask permission.

- Many flex approaches don't represent a significant change from a traditional 9-to-5 schedule. You can start at a different time, or you can do some work outside the office, but you're still basically keeping to a schedule.

- In too many firms, there's a perception that a person who is not there at the same time in the morning as everyone else is less loyal to the company.

- Most flex programs don't change the way leaders manage or assess performance. Often managers still assess employees' engagement on whether they look busy and fill up the days with meetings that create the appearance of work.

Best Buy wanted to create a fundamental change in the way employees work. The only thing employees are judged on is whether they produce results. It's flexibility plus accountability. As one leader explained, "Basically, we're rewiring people's brains, getting rid of an old belief system from the 1950s that is no longer relevant to the technologically advanced business world we have now. We want people to stop thinking of work as someplace you go to, five days a week from 8 to 5, and start thinking of work as something you do." ("Schedule Your Work Around Your Life" illustrates a case in point.)

Best Buy's approach may seem radical, but is likely to be a harbinger—in some form—of things to come.

Time-based work, and the accompanying time-based recognition and advancement that are the bedrock of our corporations today—and were essential in an industrial economy—are contrary to the needs of many. They don't work particularly well for the next several decades of your lives as Boomers. They certainly don't fit the cultural norms that are developing around the Y's. The emergence of work that is based on tasks, not time, will change all that.

## Decelerating Roles

For many people, the pressures of their current role at work are a larger issue going forward than even the time commitments. Many people would love to keep working—but not with the same level of corporate responsibility. Many would love to stay with their current firm, if there were a way to "step down"—they enjoy their colleagues and feel good

## Schedule Your Work Around Your Life

Back when he worked in a conventional corporate office for a previous employer, Best Buy employee relations manager Steve Hance admits he sometimes got through long, unproductive meetings by fantasizing about fishing or hunting. But since he began working for the Richfield, Minnesota–based national electronics retailing chain in March 2005, the outdoorsman no longer has to daydream.

Instead, when Hance participates in a morning teleconference with his coworkers or in-house clients, he sometimes is calling in via cell phone from his fishing boat on a lake or from the woods where he's spent the hours since dawn stalking wild turkeys. "No one at Best Buy really knows where I am," he explains. "Nor do they really care."

Gone are the days when Hance needed to spend from morning until night seated in a cubicle surrounded by papers and charts he'd carefully arranged to ensure that coworkers and bosses who peeked in would see he was hard at work. At Best Buy, he's free to set his own schedule, to work wherever he wants—whether it's a desk at headquarters or a table in a coffee shop—and whatever days and hours he chooses.

"It used to be that I had to schedule my life around my work," he says. "Now, I schedule my work around my life."

*Source:* Patrick J. Kiger, "Throwing Out the Rules of Work," Families and Work Institute, as quoted in *Workforce Management*, 2006, www.workforce.com.

about the company overall. But currently that opportunity does not exist for most.

From a corporate perspective, creating ways to decelerate work is an important avenue for retaining experienced, knowledgeable individuals within the company. Particularly as the possible wave of Boomer retirements triggers concerns about a rapid exodus of tacit knowledge, looking for creative ways to keep some of that know-how within the firm needs to become a high priority for many businesses. And documenting the tacit knowledge can go only so far; much of it needs to be transferred through processes similar to apprentice programs of old—hands-on interactive sharing from one generation to another.

You can help your company get creative about these possibilities. Some firms have limited, and often unimaginative, programs—the opportunity for some senior executives to remain on as "consultants"—but are finding that these constructs are of minimal value. There is a need to develop norms that allow the more "senior" executives to assume "real" positions, albeit at lower levels within the organization. There's also a need to come up with better ways to describe positions within the firms than our terminology today of "senior/junior," "higher/lower," and so on. These are all indicative of a hierarchical structure—inappropriate for the horizontally networked organizations that are likely to emerge.

Probably the best profession-wide example today is found in academia, where many of the individuals who become deans in their forties or fifties, assuming the associated leadership responsibilities, step out of that role after a period of time, returning to teaching or research. The key is that the roles they return to are not as "consultants" to the next dean— they are highly respected and valued roles in themselves.

There are few parallels in industry today, although some are emerging. There are examples in the aerospace industry of individuals who had very happily returned to the bench after several decades of management responsibility. Most reported being reenergized and highly engaged in their new "decelerated" roles.

Another story is of a senior executive who stepped out of his corporate role to take on the task of building the company's business in a small international market after his children had left the nest. Both he and his wife enjoyed the adventure of working and living in a new country; he particularly loved the opportunity to be "hands on" once again—working directly with customers and suppliers, and seeing the direct results of his efforts as the business grew. He reported being happier and more engaged than he'd felt about work in years.

One of the keys to this option, of course, is to wrestle with your Boomer tendency to worry about "how it would look." As discussed in chapter 1, many of you probably have a pretty strong competitive streak, and hierarchical roles have long been one symbol of "winning." Don't let ego stand in the way of what could be a wonderful opportunity for your third stage.

## What Else Should I Put on My List?

Hmmm . . . what will I ask for?

Start thinking of the employment deal you'd love in the broadest possible terms. Your future goals should include not only compensation, benefits, and work arrangements such as flexible schedules and deadlines, but also opportunities to learn and grow on the job. I'll argue that developing a plan for how you'll continue to learn is one of the most important elements of thinking through your next phase of work. Clearly there is no one-size-fits-all solution.

### Learning

One of the most valuable benefits continued work can provide for many Boomers is continued learning. Almost certainly, your future discussions with your employer should include a specific conversation about what you'd like to learn and ways that the company can help you achieve those goals. As you consider what you want in the way of learning, don't be constrained by conventional ideas of learning options; evaluate all of the possibilities. Learning may happen anywhere—on the job, in conversations with colleagues, through diverse assignments, or in the classroom.

Here are some possibilities:

- *Request subscriptions.* You can learn a lot from newspapers, magazines, and professional or trade journals in your leading or budding areas of interest.

- *Ask to join or form a knowledge network or community of practice within your company or community.* These communities establish connections among people who can productively teach, learn from, and share information with one another. They range from passive directories of expertise and experience (who knows what and has worked where?) to active "communities of practice" that improve individual and community knowledge and capability.

  In most firms, communities of practice are the most prolific and underleveraged channels of organizational learning—prolific because they are the most natural, inherently interorganizational and intergenerational way to transfer knowledge, and underleveraged because relatively few organizations systematically promote them. In robust knowledge networks, people know where to go for expertise and advice, and everyone is socialized to seek and share knowledge in the network. As the pace of communication and learning accelerates, the risk of brain drain (as when a very knowledgeable employee retires) diminishes, and the difficulty of tailoring training courses and assigning mentors decreases.

- *Ask to attend training programs your company may offer.* Training usually refers to activities that deliver useful content and experiences to develop specific capabilities. Courses conducted in person or virtually, plus on-the-job instruction and certification, compose most corporate training programs. Even if a capability being taught may not seem directly relevant to your current task, it may be a great skill to have in your back pocket for the future.

- *Request a continuing development plan. Development* is a broad term within organizations, generally used for processes that orchestrate work assignments, as well as training experiences to accomplish an individual's career and growth plans. In aggregate, development is intended to insure the right mix of skills and the right behaviors for meeting future needs. Unfortunately, either by your own volition or through a tactic understanding throughout a company's culture that you're about as "developed" as you're ever going to be, many of you Boomers don't participate in rigorous development planning. Make sure this isn't happening to you— ask to be included in formal development programs.[14]

- *Ask the company to fund formal educational opportunities outside work.* Formal educational programs offered by universities or industry associations can confer further certification in a field or may expand your scope and versatility (e.g., marketing for operations people).

- *Volunteer to take on an "action learning" project or other challenging special task.* Formal "action learning" experiences of the type usually associated with leadership development programs prove extremely effective. These usually combine an important, high-visibility challenge with group work on a specific business issue or problem and management review of the results. Groups combine people with various backgrounds and skills and from different parts of the organization, and the educational experience takes place in close parallel with one's regular job and responsibilities.[15]

- *Request a personal coach.* The strategic use of coaching is growing throughout corporations and extending to employees at a variety of levels. It has evolved from a punitive approach, used for "problem" employees, to a positive perk, given to high-potential leaders at a variety of levels. Coaching provides feedback and guidance in real time. Options include peer-to-peer coaches, external coaches, and coaching of teams as well as individuals.

- *Look for and request funding for relevant e-learning options.* Courseware, virtual meetings, and online discussion groups are just some of the approaches that may be available to you.

- *Request a fresh assignment.* Sadly, only about 25 percent of all workers say they're working on an exciting assignment. The percent is higher for Boomers; 35 percent of you say you're working on an exciting assignment. Even more say they're trying to cope with feelings of burnout or feeling at a dead end (see figure 4-5). A fresh assignment, often in a different location or part of an organization, lets you take advantage of your existing skills, experience, and organizational contacts while developing new ones. In some organizations, this type of internal movement across roles or units is commonplace, recognized as a facet of people's careers and valued as a means of "fresh blood circulation" throughout the enterprise.[16]

- *Request a lateral career move.* Lateral moves are a particular subset of fresh assignments that allow you to develop new skill sets, thus providing even greater scope of experience, and enhance learning more, than a new assignment based on your existing skill set. Ideally a transfer sideways would be based on some mix of new knowledge and existing strong capabilities.[17] Expect options to move laterally to become more common; with the changing shape of the workforce, vertical promotions—advancement up the

**FIGURE 4-5**

## Current conditions at work

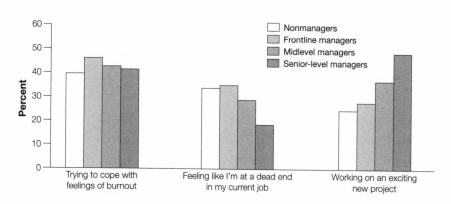

*Source: The New Employee/Employer Equation, The Concours Group and Age Wave, 2004.*

hierarchy—will occur less frequently. Career paths will be increasingly lateral—with learning as one of the key incentives.

- *Ask to be retrained for a position that is strategically critical to your company.* Some companies retrain groups of people in new roles in response to changing business conditions and skills needs. For example, in response to skills shortages in nursing, the U.K. National Health Service's "skills escalator" program trains capable employees to take the next step up the skills and job ladders, including moving from support roles into positions in patient care. Lincoln Electric's Leopard Program enabled employees to "change their spots." Rather than having to lay off workers in one part of the business while hiring others elsewhere when patterns of demand for steel fabrication products changed, the company trained factory and clerical staff volunteers to be assistant salespeople.[18]

- *Request time to work on a project of your own choosing.* Google famously allows its engineers (a large proportion of its employees) to spend up to 20 percent of their work time on projects of their choice—there is an approval process and some oversight, but the approach allows creative people to create.[19] See if your company has, or would be willing to create, a similar program, particularly if you have a burning idea that you'd like to pursue.

- *Ask to work in a customer location.* Volunteer for a stint in customer locations or customer call centers. Get out with your company's sales force. See what the world looks like from the outside in. Gain useful new perspectives for your work.

- *Offer to mentor colleagues, particularly younger workers.* Younger generational cohorts are accustomed to team learning and are comfortable working with Boomers. Putting experienced employees into mentoring, teaching, and other knowledge-sharing roles has the dual benefit of reengaging the midcareer worker and boosting the expertise and organizational know-how of less-experienced employees. For many of you, serving as a mentor may prove to be a personally fulfilling way to share a lifetime of experience, give back to the organization, and make a fresh set of social connections in the workplace.

Mentor relationships are often stereotyped as one-way transfers from old to young for the purposes of the latter's personal development and career advancement. In fact, such relationships should be viewed as a two-way pairing of individuals with knowledge to share.[20] Mentoring is a means for capitalizing on the knowledge and capability of experienced employees to develop the skills and organizational savvy of less-experienced colleagues through regular work and one-on-one consultation. But it is also an important way for the younger colleague to share their expertise, often in new technology or business techniques.[21]

- *Ask to teach in your company's in-house programs.* Most people find these roles very rejuvenating. If you're comfortable with a bit of risk, volunteer to teach something that is just slightly outside your core strength. There's no better way to master a subject than to be faced with the imminent need to explain it to others.

- *Request a sabbatical.* A sabbatical is an extended period of time away from work obligations, with the ability to rejoin the company in the same or similar capacity guaranteed. Sabbaticals can be paid or unpaid and usually last from three to twelve months. In some cases, they can be the best way to rejuvenate, personally and professionally—simply getting away from the routine of the job for a significant amount of time. People who have taken sabbaticals, whether for community service, further education, or personal endeavors, are likely to tell you that the experience was a turning point in their careers or employment relationships. An extended "career break" can help renew commitment, prevent burnout, and maintain productivity. Sabbaticals also enable employees to refresh and recharge by pursuing opportunities that are not possible during a normal training or vacation period. People return with their creative juices flowing, with fresh perspectives on how to perform work, and often with new insight into customers and markets.[22]

Whichever option appeals to you, keep in mind that learning has to do with the opportunities presented, but it is even more about your receptivity to new information—awareness, synthesis, incorporation into your existing skill sets—and the practical application of new insights. Take full advantage of all that the workplace has to offer. Learning should be one of your high priorities for this third stage of life.

## Negotiate, Barter, and Deal

As companies begin to experience the shortage of skills and talent, now is a good time to begin the process of negotiating arrangements that will work best for you.

Smart negotiating begins with understanding the lay of the land. Michael Watkins, a professor of practice at IMD and consultant on leadership, offers this checklist of things you must understand as you prepare to negotiate:[23]

- *Parties and issues:* Who is participating, and what are they negotiating about? Translated to your case, this means getting clear on who in the corporation can make what decision about your requests and preferences. What discretion does your individual manager have? What requests would need to involve others within the organization?

- *Alternatives and action-forcing events:* How do the parties see their choices and what is it that impels them to make decisions? In your case, consider what options the company has in lieu of accepting your proposal. Is there a pool of other employees with comparable skills and abilities? Are other qualified people willing to assume your responsibilities? The likelihood is increasingly slim in most companies—find out where you stand and the strength of your offering. Where are your company's potential shortages in skills and capabilities? What are your company's pivotal jobs? Where can you add the greatest value?

- *Interests and trade-offs:* What do the negotiators care about, and what trades might they be willing to make? On what metrics are the individuals who will make the decision measured? What do they care about? Many companies, for example, still have strict headcount metrics that make it difficult for managers to accept proposals for part-time work. Find out what you're up against and be prepared to discuss alternatives.

- *Information and uncertainty:* Who knows what, and what are the implications for bargaining power and strategy? This is important background for your discussions: is company management aware of the talent patterns within your business? Many companies still have not drawn a comprehensive workforce plan, and are shocked when they take a close look at their talent pipeline. Are they counting on individuals in their thirties today to step up into your role? As I discussed in chapter 1, for many members of Generation X, additional responsibility is not something they're eager to accept.

- *Positions and packages:* Who is making what demands and why? Before you begin any discussion, make sure you are very clear on what you care most about. Your dream list—things you'd love to have associated with your job—probably includes a mix of items— some that you would like, but could easily give up, and others that are just nonnegotiable. Make sure you understand which is which. And, try to find out how much flexibility the corporation has. What aspects of what you'd like are deeply rooted in corporate policy? Which ones are easy for one manager to grant?

- *Value creation and capture:* How much potential is there to create mutually-beneficial value and to capture a share of that value? Be as thorough in preparing your own proposal as you would for any business proposition. Determine the financial upside for the company of your proposal. Would you be saving the company money, perhaps in recruiting, re-training, or some other way? Increasing revenue? Providing the company with greater flexibility? Shortening the time required because you are able to accomplish something faster than a younger replacement might? What facts support your case? To the extent possible, translate the advantage of the arrangement you seek in financial terms.

As you prepare to negotiate to move to a different point on your Career Curve, gather as much insight as possible on these baseline conditions. We've discussed what corporations are likely to offer and the types of other requests you should consider for your list.

*The final key is to make sure your corporation knows what you now know:* marshal your arguments.

---

## What Will I Make Sure They Know?

Most employers today expect employees to be more informed than ever about labor markets, pay scales, and facets of the employee deal. The Internet and various online sources make it easy to find out the behind-the-scenes scoop on any corporation. Most expect that employees will be more willing than ever to shop around for the right deal and to ask for exactly what *they* want. Many are bracing, recognizing that as workforce growth slows, it will become even more of a buyer's market.[24]

But not all. Some companies and more than a few managers still believe that there will be plenty of talented individuals willing to work the old way—long hours, short vacations, rigid schedules, and fixed locations—enough to fill all the business's needs. Perhaps, but I really doubt it.

If you work in an organization that is not thinking about how to make itself more attractive to a broader range of available talent, go into your discussions prepared to provide data on the overall skills shortage and the value of retiring retirement. Marshal your best arguments.

Here's a brief recap of the highlights:

- *A growing labor shortage:* The workforce is already growing more slowly than it has in the last forty years or even declining in size in most developed markets. In the United States, the workforce is forecast to grow by only a fraction of a percentage point per year for most of the first half of the century—the total working-age population will grow at 2–3 percent per decade from now through 2030. By comparison, the growth rates were 12–15 percent per decade for most of the second half of the twentieth century. In Europe, this population will actually *decline* in size after 2010.

- *A growing skills shortage:* The workforce will not have the optimum mix of educational background, skills, and capabilities needed by rapidly emerging, knowledge-intensive industries. There will be shortages of many key skill sets. In the United States, for instance, engineering and most science disciplines are already facing critical shortages, assuming retirement ages remain unchanged. Similar patterns exist throughout much of Europe.

- *A potential leadership shortage:* The number of people between the ages of thirty-five and forty-four is declining in the United States and most industrialized countries in this decade and through 2020.

- *Boomers as a quick solution to the talent gap:* The quickest and easiest way to fill any near-term looming gap will be to continue tapping into the pool of Boomers. This group has the experience and most of the skills (okay, a little more technology training for some wouldn't hurt) to handle the jobs in the changing economy.

- *The loyalty and reliability of workers over fifty:* Boomers, as well as Traditionalists, are more likely to stay with the organization longer. There is no doubt that the younger generations are more restless at work. Today nearly a third of all Generation Y workers and a quarter of all Generation X employees say they are *actively* looking for another job at any given point in time![25] Employers on average now view over-fifty-five workers as being higher on both loyalty and reliability.[26]

- *Commitment to the organization:* Traditionalists, followed by Boomers, are significantly more likely to say that their values and the organization's are similar than other generations. They also are more likely to agree that they care about the fate of the organization and that they are willing to put in extra effort to help the organization succeed.[27]

- *Little or no extra expense, even in terms of health-care costs:* The greatest concern that employers have traditionally had about older workers has been that such workers would be too costly in terms of increased absenteeism and higher health insurance costs. These concerns, of course, are based on the perception that individuals in their sixties and seventies are "old," rather than middle aged. Today's sixty-year-old-plus workers are much healthier than those profiled even a decade ago. And the specific experience of firms employing large numbers of older workers is providing hard evidence of the misconception. Older workers have lower absenteeism; many employers have found that older workers take no more sick days than their younger counterparts.[28] Any increase in insurance premiums seems to be easily offset by increases in retention rates, customer satisfaction, and productivity.

- *Contributions to customer satisfaction and profitability:* Recall the examples from chapter 2 of the British hardware chain B&Q and U.S. drugstore chain CVS. As a generation, Boomers tend to be remarkably hardworking and productive. And as a significant percentage of the consumer economy continues to be controlled by Boomers, this cohort is well-suited to understand and meet customer needs.

- *Retention of tacit knowledge:* Today 50 percent of employers cite the loss of knowledge as their primary reaction when they contemplate the retirement of Boomers.[29] And it's a growing issue. Given the comparatively small number of X'ers in most corporations today, if the Boomers leave, even having the time to train and mentor Y's will be a challenge.

- *The benefits of flexible work arrangements:* As discussed earlier in this chapter, Best Buy's flexible work arrangements have had a significant positive impact. Employees report that they have better relationships with family and friends, feel more loyalty to the company, and feel more focused and energized about their work. And, from a business standpoint, there are financial benefits in terms of significantly lower voluntary turnover and higher productivity.

Now is the time to begin talking with employers, some of whom may not yet see the value of accommodating Boomer needs in order to engage you and keep you skills. But they soon will.

CHAPTER FIVE

# Reinvent Your Career and Your Life

## *Doing What You Want*

Thirty years, say from age fifty-five to eighty-five, is a long time. It's as long as from age twenty-five to fifty-five. It's enough time to do "it" all over again—differently, better, and with the benefit of experience and the freedom of focus. It is certainly *way* too long to keep doing something that you've already discovered you don't enjoy. If your dreams for the next stage of your life do not include continuing on with your current employer, there are many other options to consider.

Most of you will choose to spend at least some of this time in pursuit of leisure activities and enjoying your family. Some of you may want to learn skills that you've always dreamed of having time to pursue. There's no time like the present to learn to play the violin, master a new language, or delve into ancient history.

Some of you may want to pick up on your teenage intentions and spend a significant part of your newfound time working in ways that you feel give back or directly improve the world around you. Already, Boomers have the highest volunteer rate of any demographic group— nearly one-third of you volunteer in a variety of capacities.[1]

But many of you will undoubtedly use this time for new commercially oriented experiences. Some of you, perhaps particularly women, may feel a sense of personal ambition that you were not able to exercise when you were actively rearing children. You may be ready to take on more in the workplace—more responsibility, greater challenge.

Or, you may want to try a profession that you didn't attempt the first time around; thirty years is plenty of time to go to medical, nursing, or law school—and build a second, successful career. For some, your work experiences may involve entrepreneurial activities this time around—starting new businesses and pursuing ideas that have been forming in your mind throughout your "first career" experiences.

Are there types of work that would leverage your energy and abilities in new and interesting ways? Where can your skills make the biggest difference? Is there something special you still want to accomplish?

Is there a way to combine work for economic benefit with contribution to social good? Is there a cause you care deeply about? How does the idealism and yearning for meaning of your youth influence choices for your next life stage? Motivated by a life goal of making a difference, many Boomers may want to use this opportunity to craft scenarios that combine lifelong passions with the practical realities of the life they'd now like to lead.

Going forward, each of you will find activities within the broad range of newly available possibilities that will strike the deepest chord for you. Over the years ahead, you will probably end up exploring multiple different options and reconfiguring the pieces into a pattern that uniquely suits you. Work may or may not be the core activity, but it is likely to be one important—and also very gratifying—element.

What I hope you will *not* do is fall into the unfortunately all-too-common trap of allowing yourself to be bored by work—burned out, turned off, and tuned out—accepting it only as a continuing chore. Today far too many Boomers find themselves with their current employers in body, but long gone in spirit. If this is you, you are losing valuable time, an opportunity for far more enjoyment and satisfaction, and your critical edge. That's something you just can't afford—not with thirty more years ahead!

Recall the concept of *middlescence*—the process of searching for something more after a period of feeling restless, bored, or burned out with your current (midlife) activities.[2] Like adolescence, this is a critical time to take a good look at the world around you, explore some options for where you might best fit in, and build a set of skills for the next phase. For many of you, the most straightforward way to stay sharp is by finding work that is interesting, important, and personally satisfying.

Creating a brand-new path will require that you take full advantage of your second adolescence. Like teens, you need to experiment. Herminia Ibarra, in her research on how adults change careers, found that "events in their lives and work led them to envision a new range of *possible selves*, the various images—both good and bad—of whom we might become . . . "[3] She goes on to suggest, "For starters, we must reframe the questions, abandoning the conventional career-advice queries—'Who am I?'—in favor of more open-ended alternatives—'Among the many possible selves that I might become, which is most intriguing to me now? Which is easiest to test?'"[4]

This chapter's focus is on approaching the quest in ways that will help you get what you want—whatever "it" may be—whether you see your greatest ability to contribute as being in traditional industry or entrepreneurial start-ups, in the nonprofit world, through community service or the arts, through a focus on your family, or any other avenue for the famous Boomer energy. We'll look at practices to uncover and "try on" your possible selves; in each case, gauging them against the Career Curve and Life Lures frameworks that were described in chapter 3.

The three core practices for reinvention include:

1. *Explore:* Experience new people and new ideas in ways that will uncover new possibilities.

2. *Experiment:* Try new things in small steps, often while holding on to the old until you find the ones that best fit your Career Curve needs and Life Lure desires.

3. *Strengthen your edge:* Consolidate your experiences to build a strong personal reputation, while continually refreshing the leading edge that provides your greatest value.

Don't be put off by the rationale that "it"—whatever it is—would take too long. Thirty years is plenty of time. You have the time you'll need to succeed.

---

## Explore

For most of us, thinking of new and interesting things to do is difficult. Although we've all met people who were able to describe what sounded like a rational step-by-step career development path, in reality, such clarity is often crafted with the benefit of hindsight. Many of the specific individual steps were triggered by encounters along the way—people met, conversations held, observations made.

One of the best ways to find an interesting path forward is to put yourself in interesting places—in contact with interesting people—and experience the energizing shifts in behavior and attitudes under way in the world around us. Staying only within intimate circles of close friends and family may not present a full palette of alternatives; these relationships tend to preserve stability and offer familiarity.

Let's start with the quest for interesting people. Remember hearing as a child, "He who has money, makes money"? Today, that's not nearly as true. The unit of economic value is shifting. Increasingly, it's less about how much money you have, and more about how many contacts you have. The importance of financial capital is giving way to social capital. Increasingly, the biggest difference between people at the top of our economic ladder and those at the bottom is the quality of the networks they inhabit.

Networking is important for Boomers for many reasons. (See "Networking Your Way to a New Career.") Networks are a great way to connect with people with similar interests, who may be able to support a new initiative. They may comprise peers who know you well and can give you excellent, honest feedback on your ideas and activities. They are wonderful ways to stay current—with what's happening throughout your industry or profession. And, since many of the most interesting jobs are the least likely to be advertised, networking with an extended circle of colleagues, vendors, and community members, as well as family and friends, can be a key route to identifying potential opportunities. Most important, networks are probably one of the best ways to explore—to hear about new ideas, talk to people who think about the world in provocative ways, and understand more about a wide range of possibilities.

Networking should not be a chore. It is fundamentally about drawing on and nurturing connections you have made over a lifetime—and using those to form new relationships. Lynda Gratton, professor of management practice at the London Business School, uses two broad categories of relationships as a core element of her work: *strong ties*—relationships that go back years, are based on trust and reciprocity, and have an emotional element; and *weak ties*—acquaintances, people we meet less frequently, with whom we do not have a strong emotional attachment. As Gratton notes, "The truth is that new ideas and insights usually come not from strong ties but rather from the many weak ties that people have."[5]

When you're feeling stuck, one of the best approaches for moving forward is to reconfigure your network—shift your relationships, meet new people, make connections with individuals who have perspectives or experiences you do not. Develop contacts who can open doors to new worlds. Find role models and peers to guide and benchmark your progress. Surround yourself with interesting people. Put energy into joining, forming, and actively participating in networks. Try the following approaches:

- *Revitalize the many contacts you've made over your career thus far.*
  Keep track of your network. Create or update contact files.

---

## Networking Your Way to a New Career

After twenty years with AT&T, John McLaughlin, in his early sixties, was ready to leave the stress behind but was not ready to retire completely. He began discussions with two buddies, Bernie Browe and Bruce Siebert, who were the same age and who also were looking for career transitions. Each of the three identified what he wanted to do: one of John's primary goals was to do something fun and challenging with his friends. Browe wanted to leverage a Rolodex filled with high-level corporate contacts. Siebert thought he would like to leverage his networks to work in corporate premiums, like logo shirts and other sales incentive program items.

McLaughlin's network paid off when another friend, the owner of Michigan-based Gee Communications, approached John about a job promoting Gee in the Chicago area. Knowing they weren't ready to become employees again, McLaughlin and his friends formed a partnership named Gee Hilltop to help promote Gee Communications and to serve as an umbrella for whatever else they wanted to do. They used the partnership

---

Whether electronically or on paper, make sure you have up-to-date records of who is who, where they work, and how to get in touch.

- *Join a professional association.* You'll find that many of the participants have goals similar to yours and will be glad to exchange ideas and information on all sorts of career options. If possible, don't just attend the meetings; get involved by taking on a leadership role. Use these networking venues as opportunities to try out new roles, as well as to show what you can do.

- *Participate in your college's or graduate school's alumni events.* Former classmates can be some of your most powerful—and willing—contacts.

to cross-sell products and services for each other, and to mine leads where they had success.

Eventually it all came together and these three experienced and skilled executives tapped their networks for successful postretirement transitions. Gee Hilltop's Michigan-based partner was acquired. Browe and Siebert decided to continue their partnership, and McLaughlin, ready to return to employee status, joined Strategic Products and Services, where he happily manages business in two states and has eight salespeople reporting to him.

McLaughlin's new position, which involves calling on customers—something he enjoyed more than twenty years ago at the beginning of his career—has enabled him to rediscover his love of sales. Although not making as much as he did when he was responsible for 350 employees, he is happier and having fun. His network remains strong, if he decides to explore other opportunities. There's no reason to think that tapping into his network another time, for another transition, wouldn't be equally successful.

*Source:* Josh Karp, "Grumpy Old Salesmen: John McLaughlin—Age 64," http://www.retirementjobs.com/retirementstories/stories/Retirement_Stories_JohnMcLaughlin.html.

- *Look for groups to join.* Find groups that will allow you to develop relationships with people you would not typically know—clubs formed around hobbies you enjoy, charities, or community groups, for example.

- *Join an online network.* Social networks in the business world are becoming useful ways to connect colleagues and business associates. With the site Linked In, for example, you send a request to individuals you have known in the past, asking to be "linked." If they accept your invitation, you have full access to their profile, including updated contact information, both business and personal, as well as credentials such as testimonials written about them by others.[6] If you are looking for individuals with a certain capability or interest, you may search for that within the broader database, then repeat the process of requesting further contact.

Work your network. Touch base regularly—even if it's just with a brief e-mail. Ideally, provide value to your fellow network members. Networking shouldn't be a one-way street. Reciprocate—a relationship with you should be as valuable for your contact as your contact is for you. For example, if you come across an interesting article or have a relevant idea, share it with your network. Approach each individual with the mind-set, "You are important to me; I may be important to you."[7]

And don't stop at work-related opportunities. Networks can help further almost every interest. Even marriages today reflect the importance of networks in how we form communities and relationships: 12 percent of newly married couples in the United States last year were introduced to their spouses online.[8]

Networks, whether formal or informal, are not the only ways to come in contact with new ideas and possibilities. Talk with people you encounter about what they're enjoying—and what's frustrating to them. Travel to new places—with your eyes wide open. In particular, be on the lookout for things that strike you as unusual. Paul Saffo advises watching for things that don't seem to fit—they're critically important clues for the future.[9]

Perhaps one of the most important ways to explore the world today, second only to human networks, is through active use of technology. At the basic level, use it for the information it provides. Most of you are already active online—73 percent of all Boomers use the Internet at least occasionally. This, by the way, is not all that much lower than the usage levels for Gen X, at 91 percent, and Gen Y, at 86 percent—and is substantially higher than the usage level for Traditionalists at 46 percent (although even this is a healthy and rising rate, given that these folks were somewhere north of fifty before this technology became widely available).[10]

As you use the Internet, browse sites that could provide you with new ideas and possibilities to explore. For example, online job searches can give you a sense of the opportunities that are emerging as well as those where talent is in hot demand, and help you get in touch with key individuals at specific companies or in a certain geographic area.

More important, explore how the Internet and related technologies are altering the way things are getting done today. Use the new technologies. Experiment with them. Spend time around people in their teens and twenties—if you don't have children of your own, borrow some—get to know your friends' children. Watch carefully how they use technology today—what they use it for, when, and how. If you approach this thoughtfully, you'll see glimpses of new assumptions, a new culture, and new ways of operating that may present you with interesting new business possibilities.

Look for examples of the types of transformations that are under way. How will they change the way you work (and play) over the next ten years? Explore the possibilities embedded in these or other trends.

Your path for the next thirty years will be a richer journey if you travel with your eyes wide open. Put yourself in new places and with new people to garner experiences that will continually refresh and stimulate your ideas. Explore.

## Experiment

Almost no one gets it right in one big step. Changing careers—assembling a new set of satisfying activities—is an iterative process. Try something new, evaluate how well it really fits with your needs and preferences, and take another step. Experiment. Sample. Probe new possibilities. If you jump out of the workforce for a while, jump back in—at any point.

Based on your exploration, create with a long list of possibilities. Be expansive in your thinking. A broader range allows better comparison among the various avenues. It's easier to know that one option suits your interests particularly well if you've also experienced others that don't match.

I hope your explorations, coupled with the elements of the life you've already led, yield a long, long list of interesting options: activities that interest you, skills you are proud of, trends you're intrigued by, or ideas that come from watching the changes in the world. Perhaps these include things you do now, things you have always wanted to try, causes, ideas, trends:

- A form or type of expression you particularly enjoy: campaigning, selling, teaching, writing?

- Unusual patterns that you've noticed in the world: time-shifting, coordination?

- Something you've dreamed of doing: playing music, creating art, writing?

- Causes you care deeply about: the environment, opportunities for young people, political reform, the homeless?

- A favorite hobby or avocation: gardening, pets, reading?

- An unmet need in the market or, more narrowly, within your local community?

What do you do with such a list? Start to act in order to find out what to cross off and what to explore further. As Herminia Ibarra found in her work: "Once the list is done, the hard part begins: bringing some of those possible selves into the world, to evaluate them more closely."[11]

This section is about crafting experiments—finding ways to try out new activities and professional roles on a small scale before making a major commitment to the different path.

I can't offer a checklist for prioritizing and selecting from among whatever rich set of possibilities you've discovered—and will continue to unearth over the upcoming years. To find the one or ones that will form the core of your work in this next stage and to put these together into a rich life mosaic, you need to experiment and evaluate the outcome of each experiment in terms of how well the result applies to you—to your Career Curve and Life Lure.

Research conducted by my colleagues at The Concours Institute has identified five principles for experimentation.[12] These apply equally well to experiments you run in your business—and the way you approach your personal path at this point. You know it's an experiment when:

- *There is a clear experimental design or protocol.* In your personal life, this means that you need to give some conscious thought to how you might try out several of the possibilities on your list. Is there an option that would allow you to test whether it is something you really enjoy, before you plunge in with both feet? For example, could you teach a class in your community's adult education evening program before you decide to become a teacher full-time?

- *Learning objectives are stated up front.* What aspect of your second career options are you testing in each experiment? Are you trying to learn if you like working independently, on a consulting basis, or whether the specific subject area is one you enjoy—or both?

- *Listening posts are set up as a basis for organizational learning.* In your personal life, this translates into having points in the process to debrief and reflect—and ideally to obtain feedback from others. How is this working? How well does this option match the characteristics you felt were most important to your Career Curve? Does it meet the preferences expressed in your Life Lure?

- *The plan includes iterations that build on the knowledge gained in early iterations.* If you like part, but not all, of the activity, how will you modify it? For example, you may like the essential task—it may satisfy all of your Life Lure criteria—but not be comfortable with the time commitments required—it is off your Career Curve. What are the variants on this possibility that would bring it more into line?

- *Failure is an acceptable outcome of iteration.* The point, of course, is to move some things off your list—to find the things you don't want to do more of or at least not build a second career around. Therefore, failure should not only be acceptable, it may, to some extent, be the preferred outcome—at least for many of your initial possibilities.

The key is to take action. In *Surfing the Edge of Chaos*, coauthors Richard Pascale, Mark Milleman, and Linda Gioja have pointed out that "adults are much more likely to act their way into a new way of thinking than to think their way into a new way of acting."[13] And Herminia Ibarra advises that we "devote the greater part of our time and energy to action rather than reflection, to doing instead of planning."[14]

Perhaps some from the following possibilities will help stimulate additional ideas and design your own personal experiments.

## Smaller Companies

Consider moving to a company with a distinctly different work environment, perhaps one that is smaller and better able to provide you with a broader scope of activity. Being accepted by the firm on your existing strengths may provide greater opportunities to diversify—to move laterally or take on a broader scope of activity.

And you'll be part of an ongoing trend: small firms will become more prevalent over the century as a result of changes in technology, and so an increasing percentage of all employees will be employed by small firms. Research shows that small companies tend to be more attractive to employees at all levels of the organization Today, workers at small firms are on average two and a half times more highly engaged than those working for large corporations (32 percent versus 13 percent).[15] Although large employers may offer significantly greater financial benefits, the sense of engagement employees feel at small companies may prove just as attractive, if not more so.

## Consulting or Contract Work Options
## Based on Your Current Skill Set

Can your current strengths and skills provide a sufficient economic base—perhaps even enough to support other activities and experiments? There's little question that opportunities for consulting and contract work will continue to grow over the years ahead ("Cultivate Consulting Opportunities" illustrates one experience). But building a base of work is not without challenge—the need to find a continual stream of clients, refresh your knowledge, and deliver consistent value each day is critical to this option.

---

### Cultivate Consulting Opportunities

Always focused on her long-term goal of starting an herb farm when she retired, Martha Nolte needed to come up with a way to fund her dream. Relying on a professional network developed over more than twenty-five years of work as a program manager in the manufacturing and government sectors, Martha took on consulting work for income. Since Martha didn't need health insurance or other benefits, her clients were willing to pay her an excellent hourly rate, making her early retirement quite profitable. She now supplements her pension by working three days each week as a consultant, bringing her dream of an herb farm within reach.

*Source:* Joanne Murray, "Make a Late-Career Change," http://management.monster.com/articles/leveraging.

---

## Working in Different Ways
## Within Large Companies

Can you create experiments "within the system"? Can you work within a large corporation to design and try some radically new forms of work?

As I discussed in chapter 2, corporations as we know them today are still largely run along the lines established by the Traditionalists—and are not well aligned with the values of many of the individuals in this century's workforce. Our business organizations and employment policies face the significant challenge of adapting to the needs and values of the new workforce.

How can corporations evolve to become more appropriate for the workforce to come? Can you help your company change? How might you leverage your current position to reshape the hierarchical structures, rigid job designs, unilateral employment relationships, and cascading decision making that hinder the types of employer-employee relationships that many now seek? Is it possible to satisfy a desire to do work with lasting impact by doing that work on the work environment itself—creating a better corporate model for the generations to follow? Is it one of the ways—or the way—that you'll meet your life goals? Can making an impact happen through work?

## Public-Sector Activities

Over the next several decades, public-sector activities will balloon in response to the unprecedented aging of populations across the developed world. This demand for public-sector activity will call for new levels of efficiency and creativity and new gains in productivity. At the same time, the public sector, particularly the government, is likely to be one of the hardest hit segments if Boomers retire on schedule. There is a tremendous need for talented and dedicated individuals with an interest in public service.

Are there ways that you can learn more about the opportunities in this sphere, perhaps by doing some volunteer work, before moving into it on a dedicated basis?

## International Assignments Based on Your Current Skill Set

It's often possible to find short-term assignments in the international offices of law firms, financial institutions, the news media, and many other talent-starved industries ("Overseas Opportunities" provides an illustration). If there's no opportunity for transfer within your current company, see if you can arrange an unpaid leave while you experiment with a short-term assignment. Use your network—including your current employer, an alumni group, or friends overseas—to help you connect with a company abroad.

## International Work Based on Your Language Skills

Demand for English language skills is booming in many parts of Asia. Consider opportunities to teach English in China, Japan, Korea, or Taiwan. All of those countries have an almost insatiable demand for native speakers of English. Teaching jobs vary widely, but a one-year contract will probably pay you enough for rent and other living expenses. You

### Overseas Opportunities

Avi Melniker considered herself perfectly happy as a talent agent in Los Angeles until a friend raised the idea of moving to Sydney, Australia. "When she said Sydney, something inside me just went off—Sydney? I'd move to Sydney!" Within a month, Melniker was on her way to the other side of the world, where she found short-term work at a speakers' bureau. She returned several times and eventually settled in Australia, working as an events manager.

*Source:* Jane Bennett Clark, "You Call This Work?" *Kiplinger's Personal Finance*, September 2006, http://www.kiplinger.com/magazine/archives/2006/09/jobs.html.

usually don't have to speak the native language or even have teaching experience. Again, explore whether it might be possible to take a leave of absence from your current job as you experiment with this possibility.

## Transfer of One Skill to a New Venue

Is there a form of work that you do well—teaching, writing, selling? For example, if you have enjoyed selling in your previous career, worlds are opening up in online selling; for example, there are opportunities in eBay markets—as a direct seller, secondary seller, or coach for those who want to learn how. What skills have you honed that you might be able to leverage in a new arena? ("Combining Old Skills and a New Love" shows how one man applied his communications and training experience in an entirely new career.)

## Industries with Obvious Skill Shortages

The trends can help you, if you're lucky enough to have a skill set that is rapidly coming into short supply. More and more academic institutions, for example, are seeing shortages of teachers. Hospitals face an alarming shortage of nurses. Engineers are in critically short supply. And more.

These shortages will allow those of you with the requisite skills—or the willingness to learn them—tremendous leverage in creating arrangements that best suit your needs and interests. For example, hospitals are forming networks that give nurses the opportunity to work in multiple locations during seasons that appeal to them. During the winter, under this arrangement, nurses living in cold areas may elect to work in a warm climate.

## Favorite Recreational Activities or Outdoor Locations

Today, you can see the world and give your wildest fantasies legs. It is possible to land a short-term job in a dream location, from Yellowstone National Park to the Great Barrier Reef. If you want to take a mini-sabbatical or midcareer break, you can pick up extra cash while you travel. If you'd like to move to an exotic part of the world, you may find that the

## Combining Old Skills and a New Love

Howard Hayman has turned his "pet" passion into his second career—quite literally. The corporate executive who devoted decades to roles in the phone company as a customer service professional, marketer, and human resource training expert took the leap into retirement. Before long, while in the process of adopting a new puppy, he seized on the idea of becoming a professional dog trainer.

Howard's new direction was not planned. When he discovered the satisfaction of working with his dog, he entered a program to become certified as a dog trainer and behaviorist.

He had known he wanted to do something in retirement—something with flexibility—wanted to have time to experience things and have time for his interests. Now he trains dogs for hour-long sessions (three to four sessions a day), then has the rest of the day available for golfing, volunteer work, and time with his wife. He is still working hard, but on his own time—and at something he loves.

*Source:* Lisa Raffo, "Executive Dog Trainer: Howard Hayman," http://www.retirementjobs.com/retirementjobsradio.html.

job skills you already have are in big demand. Look for options at dude ranches, ski resorts, lakeside inns, mountain lodges, and national parks. These opportunities can include everything from waiting tables and mucking out stalls to leading wilderness treks and whitewater-rafting trips.

## An Environment You Enjoy

Are there people you would like to be around or worlds you'd like to be part of? Can you find a way to try out new environments? (See "Stepping into a New World" to see how one person did this.)

## Stepping into a New World

M ark Smith loved being an attorney. For twenty years he invested in his legal practice, building his reputation as an expert in Native American legal aid, consumer protection, and medical malpractice. At the height of his career, he was well known in his community for his legal work.

As he thought about his next professional steps, Smith realized that he still had a lot of energy, but wanted to spend it on something that mattered to him in a different way. After a four-month sabbatical, he had identified three things that he wanted to spend his time on, in one way or another: his love of books, his enjoyment of wine, and his passion for motorcycles.

Not knowing which direction to pursue, Smith launched a broad job search, visiting bookstores, wine shops, and motorcycle dealerships. Although some with whom he spoke were puzzled by the prospect of hiring a retiree (most were focused on bringing in younger workers), one bookstore staff member could identify with his résumé. Smith was offered a job, and has since coached the bookstore in hiring other local retirees who love books. The store now has a pool of retiree staff members, who all work part-time and cover for each others' shifts as necessary. Smith loves being around books, has established himself as an expert in a new career, and takes advantage of the new job's flexibility, which enables him to ride his motorcycle as often as he wishes. Most people he speaks with tell him, "Boy, I'd love to do something like that."

*Source:* Lisa Raffo, "Books, Wine & My Harley: Mark Smith," http://www.retirementjobs.com/retirementstories/stories/Retirement_Stories_MarkSmith.html.

## Hobbies

Some of you will discover that your next stage is less related to your former vocation than it is to an ongoing avocation—an interest or hobby you've been pursuing on your own while you've been in the working world. ("Turning the Hobby You Love into the Life You Love" gives an example.)

### Turning the Hobby You Love into the Life You Love

After thirty-two years of teaching media arts in public schools, Ed Matthews faced an important decision when his wife was diagnosed with breast cancer. At fifty-one, he wanted the freedom and flexibility to focus on her care. Although his pension would be compromised, Matthews and his wife decided to cash in on time together when it mattered most.

Once the intense days of caretaking were over and his wife was recovering, Matthews translated his love of carpentry into a business that has become a lucrative second career. "I was surprised to find that I am actually earning as much money now as when I was teaching, and I can decide to take on only those projects that I enjoy for people I want to work with and for," he says. The work also allows Matthews to control his schedule so that he can spend time with his wife.

Matthews finds himself mentoring younger workers in ways that are equally as satisfying as teaching, and he is pursuing his love of television and video production by undertaking freelance projects for area colleges and universities.

*Source:* Joanne Murray, "Make a Late-Career Change," http://management.monster.com/articles/leveraging.

## Fulfilling Societal Needs

There are many ways to make a real difference. Is there a cause—homelessness, poverty, violence, the disabled—you care deeply about? Could you begin your experiment through part-time volunteer work, and leverage it into full-time work down the road (as in the example "New Opportunity Based on a Long-Held Passion and a Lifetime Skill")?

## Emerging Economies

Look for ways to combine business skill with social good through social entrepreneurship. Many emerging-market governments will have to de-

---

### New Opportunity Based on a Long-Held Passion and a Lifetime Skill

Andrea Craig is a woman with a passion. And by combining that passion with her past work experience, she has crafted an exciting new retirement job for herself.

Craig had a successful thirty-year career as a restaurateur in Madison, Wisconsin, based on her strong love of food and cooking with local produce. But when her husband retired from his job, they decided they would enjoy the convenience and excitement of living in a dense, urban area—and moved to Manhattan.

She made several unsuccessful attempts at finding a job doing what she had been doing back in Madison, but at the same time, on a part-time basis, she kept returning to her passion for supporting and sustaining local and regional agriculture.

As Craig was contemplating her next move, her former Madison business partner, Nancy Christy, was also pondering new options—she had been approached by an organization that wanted to find a way to use its

---

cide what level of social services to provide to citizens who increasingly demand state-provided protections such as health care and retirement security. The adoption of proven private-sector approaches will likely become pervasive in the provision of social services in both the developed and the developing worlds.[16]

## Fulfilling a Local Need

In addition to looking at the broader trends, don't neglect singular needs close to home. What is happening in your local community? Is there a need that would be satisfying to fill? ("A 'Need-based' Career Switch" tells of one such opportunity.)

existing kitchen facilities to generate income and teach job skills to the homeless. Christy also had a long-standing personal commitment to providing opportunities for the disabled.

Craig and Christy put their heads together and came up with a proposal that addressed their multiple passions. The kitchen would employ homeless people and the disabled to produce two or three "value-added" products that would help local farmers by using local ingredients. A Madison philanthropist funded a feasibility study. And recently the Madison Community Foundation awarded a grant to fund the creation of the business plan.

Craig feels that while this is a big change for her—it's not jumping into something completely new. "It's seamless in a way," she reflects. "Doing something you care about, any aggravations kind of drop away."

Her passion still fuels her work now as much, if not more, than it did from the very beginning. "I wasn't ready to not contribute. I felt like I should be still out there," she explains. "We're all in this together and there's a lot that needs to be done."

*Source:* Lisa Raffo, "Giving Back: The Andrea Craig Story," http://www.retirementjobs.com/retirementstories/stories/Retirement_Stories_AndreaCraig.html.

---

## A "Need-Based" Career Switch

Embracing the idea that the key to a happy retirement is to retire in a location you love, Liz Vallard chose her retirement destination of Martha's Vineyard first, and then worried about how to fund that choice. Although she had been a former college professor, Vallard, now in her early sixties, was willing to do whatever it took to stay on Martha's Vineyard. Her first jobs included work as a technical lighting designer in a theater and a tour guide. She then became involved in a discussion about the need for a ferry captain, and passed the qualifying test with ease. Vallard now works as a ferry captain full-time and has happily settled into life on Martha's Vineyard, her dream location.

*Source:* Lisa Raffo, "Professor and Captain: Liz Vallard," http://www.retirementjobs.com/retirementstories/stories/Retirement_Stories_LizVallard.html.

---

After each experiment, take time to debrief—how well did it match your Career Curve and Life Lure?

And don't be discouraged. Take to heart Herminia Ibarra's observation: "Almost no one gets change right on the first try."[17]

---

## Strengthen Your Edge

This last section is about the benefits of consolidation and the dangers of complacency.

One other important trend in the world in which you'll live this third stage of life is a shift in the way individual performance is measured and ranked. You grew up in a world in which your achievements were typically evaluated by someone in authority or with expertise. Going forward, this approach will decrease in importance, to be replaced by reputation built through a broad consensus of judgments made by your peers regarding your capabilities and contributions.

Sound scary? It can be, to those who are used to playing a game with a very different set of rules.

This next stage of your life is going to occur in a world in which building your reputation will be the key skill for consolidating your success. At the same time, whatever reputation you enjoy today will have an increasingly short half-life. Maintain your edge. Avoid complacency.

## Consolidate: Build Your Brand

Understanding the growing importance of reputation requires understanding the central role that networks of peer-to-peer activity play. Knowledge acquisition, for example, increasingly has a peer-to-peer element—as opposed to the more hierarchical authority-to-learner model that many Boomers still follow. Why? Because there is *so much* information available today that it's very difficult to know which sources to trust. Increasingly you'll begin the knowledge acquisition process by touching base with peers—either to obtain information directly or identify peer-vetted sources.

Peer networks are hierarchy-free. They do not take into account formal titles or positions; they run on acknowledged expertise. When new knowledge is obtained, it is not sent *up* any formal chain of command to be approved; rather it is posted *broadly* or sent, via the network, to people who are believed to be most interested or most in the need to know. Similarly, questions are not directed to supervisors who control the flow of knowledge, but to people at all levels who have proven reliable sources in the past.

These same principles will increasingly play out in the world of work. As a result, your reputation will be critically important—whether online or in the real world. As you begin to home in on the central activities of your evolving life, it will be important to look for ways to pull the threads together—to consolidate the themes of your activities into what is essentially a personal "brand."

Your contribution will increasingly be measured and valued through the opinion of your peers. Evaluation by a "superior" or a positional authority will become almost unheard-of. As your contributions are increasingly measured and valued through the opinion of your peers, and evaluation by positional authorities grows less important, being the "teacher's pet" or "currying favor with the boss" may become foreign concepts.

Again, consider the world of gaming, which today is heavily based on this peer-evaluation model. In the highly popular *World of Warcraft*, participants are reviewed in postbattle debriefings by fellow guild members; the outcome of this peer judgment is more important to players' progress in the game than the number of battle awards they have received. In *Warcraft*, participants use peer assessments to identify which person in the guild can be most helpful in each specific future encounter. But gaming is not the vanguard of this system—guilds of the Middle Ages and most professional service firms today are characterized by heavy elements of peer evaluation.

In peer-to-peer systems, it is not enough to have a positive reputation for your work—having credibility as a critic is important as well. The community rates those who rate. One's value as a critic is key, for example, on Amazon, where the reputation of the reviewer can be seen in its collaborative filtering referral system.

The process of building your brand begins with understanding your unique value and how to refresh it.

One of my favorite personal development books is one that was not written for the individual: it's Jim Collins' *Good to Great*, written to help corporations understand the ingredients of greatness. In it, Collins describes what he calls the "hedgehog" concept which takes its name from the old Greek adage, "The fox knows many things, but the hedgehog knows one big thing." It means finding the intersection of something the company has the capability to be the best in the world at, that its leaders enjoy passionately, *and* that the company can make money at. Companies that find the intersection of these three circles, in Jim's research, go on to be "great." Collins argues that being a hedgehog is the first and most important step on a company's path to success.[18]

In the same book, Collins also describes the importance of the flywheel as an image for sustained success. As he says: "Good to great comes about by a cumulative process—step by step, action by action, decision by decision, turn by turn of the flywheel—that adds up to sustained and spectacular results."[19]

This same smart advice obviously also applies to you as an individual. Becoming a "hedgehog" and developing a step-by-step, day-after-day way to turn your own "flywheel" is critical to your future success. To do that, you need to become essentially a product manager for your own skills and capabilities. Think of *yourself* as the product you're selling (or volunteering) to the marketplace. And, just as a product manager would be concerned with understanding, communicating, and leveraging the existing brand equity while continually renewing and refreshing the product attributes—always searching for "new and improved"—do the same for yourself.

First, figure out the essential core of your brand. Start looking for that sweet spot that represents your unique strengths, special passions, and practical realities. As you think about your brand, remember—it does not have to be a specific area of knowledge. It may include "soft" attributes, such as your dependability, enthusiasm, motivation, flexibility, and people orientation. What comes to your colleagues' minds when they think of you?

Whatever you determine to be your brand, try to capture it in language that represents others' perceptions and feelings about the product—in this case, about you. Brand positioning involves making what you're all about clear in others' minds. Imagine that someone was going to do a Google search to find you—what key words would you want to lead to your name? Create your "tag line"—language that captures the essence of your brand. The clearer you can make this in your mind, the better able you will be to build and reinforce it throughout all your related activities.

## Avoid Complacency

No one is saying it will be easy. There will be opportunities—possibilities—but capturing them will require discipline, preparation, and continual learning to stay on the edge where value is created.

Many of the work styles I've discussed will take more organization and discipline than working within one firm. You have to manage not just doing the work, but marketing and selling your skills, customer service, and all invoicing and collection issues. Keeping them all in balance will be a challenge. The most difficult part of cyclic work is getting so immersed in one cycle that you spend no time or thought on the next. Set aside time each day, or at least each week, or focus on "what's next."

Create the context for discipline. Develop a disciplined schedule. Arrange a home office or other suitable work space. Identify options for appropriately professional support.

Stay up-to-date on the latest thinking in your area of expertise. Renew any relevant certifications or licenses; do not allow them to lapse. One of the outcomes of increasing cyclic work will be the growing demand for certification, whether externally, to establish cross-company norms, or internally, as part of a process of validation for executive readiness. Consider working within your profession, industry, or skill base to establish cross-company certifications that will quickly and easily communicate to others your degree of proficiency in a given field.

Develop a "product development" strategy for investments in yourself. Identify the edges of your expertise—where are things changing the fastest? Where are your current capabilities likely to become obsolete? Develop a learning strategy; select several ways of learning—for example, participating in formal education, experiencing new things, and putting yourself in situations that will challenge and extend your capabilities—that you'll incorporate into your work this year. With your unique edge in mind, invest in yourself to insure that you continue to have high-value capabilities in a rapidly evolving knowledge economy.

But don't stop there. Whatever you've pinpointed will need to grow and be constantly refreshed to remain unique tomorrow.

*Bottom line:* expect that your best knowledge, skills, or capabilities today will become commodities tomorrow. Recognize that you are one participant in a global knowledge evolution. Think about your leading edge— what are your most differentiated and valuable skills today? What do you need to learn to make sure that you continue to have differentiated and high value skills in the future? (See "Pushing Up the Knowledge Ladder.")

## Pushing Up the Knowledge Ladder

In *The World Is Flat*, Tom Friedman tells the story of his childhood friend Bill Greer, a freelance artist and graphic designer who worked with clients such as the *New York Times* in pretty much the same way for twenty years. For all of those years, Bill produced camera-ready art—physical pieces that would then be photographed and prepared for publication. But beginning in about 2000, his world began to shift—to digital preparation. Aided by sophisticated software, graphic design became a commodity—all of a sudden anyone could produce an acceptable-quality product.

Greer pushed himself up the "knowledge ladder," looking for work that his experience and talent would allow him to do, that young artists couldn't do equally well with technology for half the price. He moved into "ideation"—sketching creative concepts that then could be finished or illustrated by lower-paid individuals using computer programs.

Then the technology evolved further and, at the request of one of his clients, Greer used the latest technology to develop a specialization in "morphs"—a cartoon strip in which one character evolves into another. At the last telling, he was successfully working in this specialized area—but with one eye out for the next step up the ladder.

*Source:* Thomas L. Friedman, *The World Is Flat: A Brief History of the Twenty-first Century* (New York: Farrar, Straus and Giroux, 2006), 240–243.

Although some people associate "career change" with something radical and therefore risky—jumping the corporate ship to pursue a passion or an avocation—the notion of a single career is becoming obsolete. A midcareer change is becoming a sign of success in adapting, not failure to thrive in one's original occupation.[20] You have a second chance to be a star, to do something you love. Pick something you care about, and go for it!

You are the Boomers: you have repeatedly reshaped your lives and fueled much of the productivity of the last several decades—and you will continue to do so for decades to come. Now you will harness your next decades of productive capacity—in traditional work or in a less conventional application of your skills. The choice is yours. The opportunities you choose should fit your own special needs, unique talents, and personal passions.

Turn your conjectures about the future you'd like to live into conviction—and then, concrete reality.

Have a wonderful thirty, or more, years!

# NOTES

## Introduction

1. Dr. Peter Markiewicz, "Who's Filling Gen Y's Shoes?" Brand Channel.com, May 5, 2003, http://www.brandchannel.com/features_effect.asp?pf_id=156. (Quoting research conducted by the Gallup Organization.)

2. Ken Dychtwald, Tamara J. Erickson, and Robert Morison, *Workforce Crisis: How to Beat the Coming Shortage of Skills and Talent* (Boston: Harvard Business School Press, 2006).

3. Peter F. Drucker, "Managing Knowledge Means Managing Oneself," *Leader to Leader*, no. 16 (Spring 2000): 8–10.

4. Herminia Ibarra, *Working Identity: Unconventional Strategies for Reinventing Your Career* (Boston: Harvard Business School Press, 2003).

5. Edgar H. Schein, *Career Anchors: Discovering Your Real Values*, rev. ed. (San Diego, CA: University Associates, 1990).

6. Ibarra, *Working Identity*.

7. Ibid.

## Chapter One

1. Formative work in this area includes that done by Morris Massey, "What You Are Is Where You Were When," training video (Cambridge, MA: Enterprise Media, 1976); and Neil Howe and William Strauss, *Generations: The History of America's Future, 1584 to 2069* (New York: Harper Collins, 1992).

2. Drills held in most schools in preparation for nuclear attacks. They were often described to the children as "tornado drills" or masked under some other perplexing guise.

3. *The First Measured Century: The Other Way of Looking at American History*, videocassettes, Public Broadcasting System, 2000.

4. Ibid.

5. Ibid.

6. John T. Molloy, *Dress for Success* (New York: P.H. Wyden, 1975).

7. Greenberg Quinlan Rosner/Polimetrix, "Coming of Age in America, Part III," Research Report, January 2006, p. 3, http://www.greenbergresearch.com.

8. Re.sults Project YE, *Engaging Today's Young Employees: Strategies for the Millennials*, The Concours Institute, a member of BSG Alliance, 2007.

# Notes

9. Louise Story, "Many Women at Elite Colleges Set Career Path to Motherhood," *New York Times*, September 20, 2005.

10. Sylvia Ann Hewlett and Carolyn Buck Luce, "Off-Ramps and On-Ramps: Keeping Talented Women on the Road to Success," *Harvard Business Review*, March 2005, 43–54.

11. Neil Howe, William Strauss, and R. J. Matson (illustrator), *Millennials Rising: The Next Great Generation* (New York: Vintage Books, 2000).

12. Dr. Peter Markiewicz, "Who's Filling Gen Y's Shoes?" Brand Channel.com, May 5, 2003, http://www.brandchannel.com/features_effect.asp?pf_id=156. (Quoting research conducted by the Gallup Organization.)

13. Ibid., quoting research conducted by Applied Research & Consulting LLC.

14. "The New Employee/Employer Equation," The Concours Group and Age Wave, 2004. This research project included a nationwide survey of over seventy-seven hundred employees conducted in June 2004 by Harris Interactive for The Concours Group and Age Wave.

15. "The 2006 Cone Millennial Cause Study: The Millennial Generation: Pro-Social and Empowered to Change the World," Cone, Inc., in collaboration with AMP Insights, October 2006.

16. "Generation 2001: A Survey of the First College Graduating Class of the New Millennium," poll conducted by Louis Harris & Associates, Inc., on behalf of Northwestern Mutual Life Insurance, February 1998.

17. Re.sults@Project YE, *Engaging Today's Young Employees: Strategies for the Millennials*, The Concours Institute, a member of BSG Alliance, 2007.

18. Robert Morison, Tamara J. Erickson, and Ken Dychtwald, "Managing Middlescence," *Harvard Business Review*, March 2006, 78–86.

19. Ibid.

20. Deborah Rothberg, "Non-Retiring 'Retirees' Fastest-Growing Job Market Sector," *eWeek*, September 22, 2006, http://www.careers.eweek.com/print_article/NonRetiring+Retirees+FastestGrowing+Job+Market+Sector/189355.aspx.

21. "TV Land's New Generation Gap Study," Age Wave and Harris Interactive, 2006. TV Land, a unit of Viacom's MTV Networks, engaged Age Wave to design this landmark study to develop a new understanding of the Boomers in their power years and their expectations of and relationship to television and advertising. This study included a national survey of 4,220 adults conducted online by Harris Interactive.

22. Ibid.

## Chapter Two

1. "Boardroom Imperative: Next Generation Enterprises," paper, BSG Concours, a division of BSG Alliance, Inc., 2007.

2. "Meeting the Challenges of Tomorrow's Workplace," *Chief Executive*, August–September, 2002.

3. "Population Projections 2004–2050," press release, Eurostat, April 8, 2005.

4. "2006 Education at a Glance: OECD Indicators," 2006 edition, Centre for Educational Research and Innovation, 2006, http://www.oecd.org/document/52/0,3343,en_2649_201185_37328564_1_1_1_1,00.html.

5. Seventh-Annual Workplace Report, "Challenges Facing the American Workplace, Summary of Findings," Employment Policy Foundation, 2002.

6. *Education at a Glance: OECD Indicators*, (Paris: OECD, 2006).

7. Gary Orfield, ed., *Dropouts in America: Confronting the Graduation Rate Crisis* (Cambridge, MA: Harvard Education Press, 2004).

8. "Dropouts in California: Confronting the Graduation Rate Crisis," research report, The Civil Rights Project, Harvard University, 2006.

9. *The First Measured Century: The Other Way of Looking at American History*, videocassettes, Public Broadcasting System, 2000.

10. Anne Fisher, "Holding on to Global Talent," *Fortune*, October 19, 2005.

11. "Networking Skills in Europe: Will an Increasing Shortage Hamper Competitiveness in the Global Market?" IDC White Paper, sponsored by Cisco Systems, September 2005.

12. For a more extensive discussion of the formation of "hot spots," see Lynda Gratton, *Hot Spots: Why Some Teams, Workplaces, and Organizations Buzz with Energy—and Others Don't* (San Francisco: Berrett-Koehler, 2007).

13. Re.sults@Project YE, *Engaging Today's Young Employees: Strategies for the Millennials*, The Concours Institute, a member of BSG Alliance, 2007.

14. Ibid.

15. Paul Saffo, personal conversation with author, May 2007.

16. http://www.irobot.com.

17. http://en.wikipedia.org/wiki/Robot.

18. James Surowiecki. *The Wisdom of Crowds: Why the Many Are Smarter Than the Few and How Collective Wisdom Shapes Business, Economics, Societies, and Nations* (New York: Doubleday, 2004), xiiv.

19. Howard Rheingold, *Smart Mobs: The Next Social Revolution* (New York: Perseus Publishing, 2005), 31.

20. Saffo, personal conversation.

21. Thomas W. Malone, *The Future of Work: How the New Order of Business Will Shape Your Organization, Your Management Style, and Your Life* (Boston: Harvard Business School Press, 2004).

22. Emily Stover De Rocco, "Skills Development for the 21st Century," speech delivered at the Workplace Learning Conference, December 8, 2003, http://www.doleta.gov/whatsnew/Derocco_speeches/Workplace_Learning.cfm.

23. Peter F. Drucker, "The Next Society," *The Economist*, November 3, 2001.

24. "Life Expectancy at Birth, 65 and 85 Years of Age, by Sex and Race: United States, Selected Years 1900–2003 (LIFEX03a)." National Center for Health Statistics, http://209.217.72.34/aging/TableViewer/tableView.aspx?ReportId=357.

25. Carrie Sturrock, "We're Living Longer—Is That a Good Thing?" *San Francisco Chronicle*, March 6, 2006, http://www.sfgate.com/cgi-bin/article.cgi?file=/c/a/2006/03/06/MNGICHJ8311.DTL.

26. Bruce J. Klein, "This Wonderful Lengthening of Lifespan," *The Longevity Meme*, January 17, 2003, http://www.longevitymeme.org/articles.

27. Edward E. Potter, testifying before the Special Committee on Aging of the U.S. Senate, September 20, 2004, cited in Ken Dychtwald, Tamara J. Erickson, and Robert

Morison, *Workforce Crisis: How to Beat the Coming Shortage of Skills and Talent* (Boston: Harvard Business School Press, 2006), 5.

28. Stefan Theil, "The New Old Age: Retirees Go Back to Work," *Newsweek International*, January 30, 2006.

29. "CVS Pharmacy Receives Top Honor for Mature Worker Initiatives 2007," press release (CSRwire), March 9, 2007, http://www.csrwire.com/News/7778.html.

30. Challenger Gray & Christmas, September 2006. Source: "Older Workers Gain Jobs Fastest; Boomer Competition Could Slow Growth," press release, September 27, 2006, http://www.interbiznet.com/bugler/bugler_06.09.27.html.

31. "The Future of Retirement Study," HSBC, 2005.

32. Deborah Rothberg, "Non-Retiring 'Retirees' Fastest-Growing Job Market Sector," *eWeek*, September 22, 2006, http://www.careers.eweek.com/print_article/NonRetiring+Retirees+FastestGrowing+Job+Market+Sector/189355.aspx.

33. "The Working Retired," Putnam Investments, 2005.

34. *OECD Factbook 2007: Economic, Environmental and Social Statistics* (Paris: OECD, 2007).

35. "The New Employee/Employer Equation," The Concours Group and Age Wave, 2004.

36. Theil, "The New Old Age."

37. "The Retirement Prospects of the Baby Boomers," Congressional Budget Office, Economic and Budget Issue Brief, March 18, 2004, http://www.cbo.gov/ftpdoc.cfm?index=5195&type=0.

38. "The Future of Retirement Study," HSBC, 2005.

39. Ibid.

40. See *The Millennials: Americans Born 1977 to 1994*, 3rd ed. (Ithaca, NY: New Strategist Publications, 2006); and U.S. Census Bureau, "A Child's Day: 2000 (Selected Indicators of Child Well-Being)," August 2003.

41. Patty Giordani, "'Y' Recruiting: New Generation Inspires New Methods," *NACE Journal* 65, no. 4 (Summer 2005): 23–25.

42. "A Portrait of 'Generation Next': How Young People View Their Lives, Futures and Politics," study released by The Pew Research Center for the People and the Press, January 2007.

43. Pamela Paul, "The PermaParent Trap," *Psychology Today*, September–October 2003, http://psychologytoday.com/articles/index.php?term=pto-20030902-000002&page=1.

44. Ben Grill, quoted in "Teen Trends: Inside the Minds of Today's Teens," *Partnership for a Drug-Free America*, http://www.drugfree.org/Parent/Knowing/Teen_Trends.

45. "Adventure Travel Report," *TIA Publications*, February 1998.

46. William Damon, "The Gap Generation" *USAWeekend.com*, April 29, 2001, http://www.usaweekend.com/01_issues/010429/010429teens.html.

47. Sharon Jayson, "Gen Y Makes a Mark and Their Imprint Is Entrepreneurship," *USA Today*, December 8, 2006, http://www.usatoday.com/news/nation/2006-12-06-gen-next-entrepreneurs_x.htm.

48. Paul, "The PermaParent Trap."

*Notes*

## Chapter Three

1. "Fact Sheet on Older Americans," Civic Ventures, June 2000, http://www.civicventures.org/publications/articles/fact_sheet_on_older_americans.cfm.
2. "The Future of Retirement Study," HSBC, 2005.
3. "Re-Visioning Retirement Study" AIG SunAmerica, 2006.
4. Herminia Ibarra, *Working Identity: Unconventional Strategies for Reinventing Your Career* (Boston: Harvard Business School Press, 2003).
5. "The New Employee/Employer Equation," The Concours Group and Age Wave, 2004.
6. Martha Finney, personal conversation with author, March 2007.
7. Families and Work Institute, "Generation & Gender in the Workplace," American Business Collaboration, 2004, http://familiesandwork.org/eproducts/genandgender.pdf.
8. Mihaly Csikszentmihalyi, *Finding Flow: The Psychology of Engagement with Everyday Life* (New York: Basic Books, 1997).
9. Research findings in this section from "The New Employee/ Employer Equation." For further information, see Ken Dychtwald et al., *Handbook of the New American Workforce* (Kingwood, TX: The Concours Group, 2006).
10. Edgar H. Schein, *Career Anchors: Discovering Your Real Values*, rev. ed. (San Diego, CA: University Associates, 1990).
11. Tamara J. Erickson and Lynda Gratton, "What It Means to Work Here," *Harvard Business Review*, March 2007, 104–112.

## Chapter Four

1. Jody Miller and Matt Miller, "Get A Life! Ditching the 24/7 Culture," *Fortune*, November 16, 2005.
2. Sylvia Ann Hewlett and Carolyn Buck Luce, "Off-Ramps and On-Ramps: Keeping Talented Women on the Road to Success," *Harvard Business Review*, March 2005, 43–54.
3. Re.sults Project YE, *Engaging Today's Young Employees: Strategies for the Millennials*, The Concours Institute, a member of BSG Alliance, 2007.
4. Ken Dychtwald, Tamara J. Erickson, and Robert Morison, *Workforce Crisis: How to Beat the Coming Shortage of Skills and Talent* (Boston: Harvard Business School Press, 2006).
5. Quoted in Miller and Miller, "Get A Life!"
6. Dychtwald, Erickson, and Morison, *Workforce Crisis*.
7. Ibid.
8. Patrick J. Kiger, "Throwing Out the Rules of Work," *Workforce Management*, 2006, www.workforce.com.
9. "The Future of Retirement Study," HSBC, 2005, 6.
10. Marco R. della Cava, "Working Out of a 'Third Place,'" *USA Today*, October 5, 2006.
11. Ibid.
12. Dychtwald, Erickson, and Morison, *Workforce Crisis*.

13. Kiger, "Throwing Out the Rules of Work."

14. Dychtwald, Erickson, and Morison, *Workforce Crisis.*

15. Ibid.

16. Ibid.

17. Robert Morison, Tamara J. Erickson, and Ken Dychtwald, "Managing Middlescence," *Harvard Business Review*, March 2006, 78–86.

18. Dychtwald, Erickson, and Morison, *Workforce Crisis.*

19. Eric Schmidt and Hal Varian, "Google: Ten Golden Rules" *Newsweek*, December 2005, http://www.msnbc.msn.com/id/10296177/site/newsweek/.

20. Morison, Erickson, and Dychtwald, "Managing Middlescence."

21. Dychtwald, Erickson, and Morison, *Workforce Crisis.*

22. Ibid.

23. Michael Watkins, *Shaping the Game: The New Leader's Guide to Effective Negotiating* (Boston: Harvard Business School Press, 2006).

24. Dychtwald, Erickson, and Morison, *Workforce Crisis.*

25. "The New Employee/Employer Equation," The Concours Group and Age Wave, 2004.

26. "The Future of Retirement Study."

27. Ibid.

28. Challenger Gray & Christmas, September 2006. Source: "Older Workers Gain Jobs Fastest; Boomer Competition Could Slow Growth," press release, September 27, 2006, http://www.interbiznet.com/bugler/bugler_06.09.27.html.

29. "The Future of Retirement Study."

## Chapter Five

1. "Baby Boomers and Volunteering: An Analysis of the Current Population Survey," Corporation for National and Community Service and RTI International Issue Brief, 2005.

2. Robert Morison, Tamara J. Erickson, and Ken Dychtwald, "Managing Middlescence," *Harvard Business Review*, March 2006, 78–86.

3. Hazel Markus and Paula Nurius, "Possible Selves," *American Psychologist* 41, no. 9 (1986): 954–969, as quoted in Herminia Ibarra, *Working Identity: Unconventional Strategies for Reinventing Your Career* (Boston: Harvard Business School Press, 2003), 13.

4. Ibarra, *Working Identity*, 35.

5. Lynda Gratton, *Hot Spots: Why Some Teams, Workplaces, and Organizations Buzz with Energy—and Others Don't* (San Francisco: Berrett-Koehler, 2007), 72.

6. www.linkedin.com.

7. David Corbett with Richard Higgins, *Portfolio Life: The New Path to Work, Purpose and Passion After 50* (San Francisco: Jossey-Bass, 2007).

8. Ian Davis and Elizabeth Stephenson, "Ten Trends to Watch in 2006," *McKinsey Quarterly*, Web exclusive, January 2006.

9. Paul Saffo, "Six Rules for Effective Forecasting," *Harvard Business Review*, July 2007, 122–131.

10. "How Young People View Their Lives, Futures, and Politics: A Portrait of Generation Next," study released by The Pew Research Center for the People and the Press, January 2007.

11. Herminia Ibarra, *Working Identity: Unconventional Strategies for Reinventing Your Career* (Boston: Harvard Business School Press. 2003), 41–42.

12. Re.sults Project TBE, *Techniques for Business Experimentation*. The Concours Group, March 2005.

13. Richard T. Pascale, Mark Milleman, and Linda Gioja, *Surfing the Edge of Chaos: The Laws of Nature and the New Laws of Business* (New York: Crown Business, 2000).

14. Ibarra, *Working Identity*, xi.

15. "The New Employee/Employer Equation," The Concours Group and Age Wave, 2004.

16. Davis and Stephenson, "Ten Trends to Watch in 2006."

17. Ibarra, *Working Identity*, 168.

18. Jim Collins, *Good to Great*, 1st ed. (New York: Harper Collins, 2001).

19. Ibid.

20. Ken Dychtwald, Tamara J. Erickson, and Robert Morison, *Workforce Crisis: How to Beat the Coming Shortage of Skills and Talent* (Boston: Harvard Business School Press, 2006).

# INDEX

*Note:* Page numbers followed by *f* indicate figures; page numbers followed by *t* indicate tables.

social movement toward, 53–54
technology and, 47–48, 49, 52
college(s)
decelerating roles in academia, 119
networking at alumni events, 138
new uses of technology by, 51
rates of graduation, 44, 45*f*
college degrees, skills gap and, 44
Collins, Jim, 156–157
commitment to change, 14
communal relationships in workplace, 35
communication, engagement and, 90, 96–97
communities of practice, 120
compensation. *See also* benefit packages
bell-shaped curve and, 107
effects on engagement, 90, 96–97
income less important to Gen Y, 68, 84
limited obligations archetype and, 96
monetary reward as motivation, 18
"peak wage" contracts, 107
competitiveness of Boomers, 12–13
complacency, avoiding, 158–160
compressed workweek, 110
Concours Institute, The, 35, 143
connection, engagement and, 90–91, 96–97
construction industry, 57–58
"consultant" positions, 119
consulting, experimentation in, 145
consumerism, 16, 17*f*
"creator-consumers," 55–56
individual choice and, 48
in workforce, 106
consumer society of 1950–2000, 53
content, effects on engagement, 90, 96–97
continuing development plan, 121–122
continuous partial attention, 29
contract work, 145
conventional flextime, 106–107, 116–117
"coordinating," 51–52
co-purchase decisions, 68

core work options, 5–6
corporate policies. *See* human resource policies
corporate restructuring, 21–22
corporations
alignment with individual, 48
changes in, opportunity and, 55–56, 146
differences in components of work experience, 91
experimentation within system, 146
need to adapt to flexible work, 48–49
perspectives of deceleration, 118–119
policies of (*see* human resource policies)
predictable path of corporate work, 77, 78*f*
problem of loss of talent, 49, 77
rigid schedules in, 50
run by views of Traditionalists, 14, 15, 146
taboos in corporate culture, 104
willingness to offer options, 72
cost savings, from virtual work, 115
"crafting experiments," 7
Craig, Andrea, 152–153
creativity
collaborative work and, 53
entrepreneurial (career anchor), 97, 98
need for, 5
"creator-consumers," 55–56
creator economy of 2000 onward, 53–54
Csikszentmihalyi, Mihaly, 87
customer-facing archetype (Career Curve), 85, 86*t*
customer satisfaction, 61, 130–131
customization, individual choice and, 48
CVS, 62, 130–131
cyclic time, 109, 112*f*, 112–113, 113*f*
cyclic work
demographics of, 113, 113*f*
focus on "what's next" and, 158
negotiating, 7

Index

# ABOUT THE AUTHOR

**Tamara Erickson** is both a respected, McKinsey Award–winning author and popular and engaging storyteller. Her compelling views of the future are based on extensive research on changing demographics and employee values and, most recently, on how successful organizations work. Well grounded, academically rigorous, and fundamentally optimistic, Tammy's work discerns and describes interesting trends in our future and provides actionable counsel to help both organizations and individuals prepare for these trends today.

Tammy has coauthored four *Harvard Business Review* articles, one *MIT Sloan Management Review* article, and the book *Workforce Crisis: How to Beat the Coming Shortage of Skills and Talent*. She is President of The Concours Institute, a member of BSG Alliance (www.BSGAlliance.com), a firm supporting senior executives with an integrated platform of strategic research, leadership development, expert advisory services, on-demand software solutions, and technology professional services. Tammy's weekly blog "Across the Ages" is available on HBSP Online (http://discussionleader.hbsp.com/erickson/).

You can reach Tammy at www.TammyErickson.com.